OCTOBER

IN MY SOUL

Sonja Carlo

Copyright © 2012 Sonja Carlo

All rights reserved.

ISBN:1480277134
ISBN-13:9781480277137

For my grandchildren,
James Wells, Nikita Strozewski, Carrie Routh, Ronald Strozewski, Jacqueline Strozewski, David Routh, Savannah Strozewski, Ciara Strozewski, Brandi Strozewski, and Zachary Strozewski. I want especially to leave them these things, the things I never told them that they need to know.

CONTENTS

    Acknowledgments   i

1	The Rooting 1939	1
2	Art's Girls	5
3	Churches	12
4	High School	21
5	Ronnie	26
6	The Snoopy Gospel	30
7	Mysterious	34
8	Enter Fiend	38
9	My Skin Crawls	42
10	Full Of Grace	46
11	Stilled And Beheld	49
12	A Second Encounter	53
13	When Kim Is 21	58
14	The Aftermath	62
15	Kim	68
16	October Listening	73
17	Flashbacks	79
18	Puzzle Pieces	83
19	Loose Ends	87
20	The Comforter Speaks	91
21	Holy Is His Name	95
22	Time To Mourn	102
23	Enter November	106
24	Even He	112

October In My Soul

ACKNOWLEDGMENTS

I am immensely grateful to my daughter Ann Routh, and granddaughter Carrie Ann Routh, both teachers, who read, edited, and critiqued the first rough but completed manuscripts. They gave me ongoing affirmation and encouragement. My daughter Ann was instrumental in encouraging me to get this written by wanting me to tell this on a video for her one summer a few years ago. I am indebted also to my friend Sandy Fleming, for help with my website and manuscript editing who, besides being my website tutor is also a teacher, language tutor, and a self published author. Laryssa Baczynskyj, Karen Camp, Pauline Maurer, all friends and members of the prayer group, greatly helped with editing and polishing and encouragement of the final proofs of the book. In addition to those mentioned the comments and thoughts from my grandson Ronald Strozewski, who read and edited one of the final proofs, were extremely valuable in getting this book on the road to being published. But without the prayers and encouragement of The Servants of the Lord Jesus Christ Prayer Group, I would never have been able to bring this to conclusion, as I struggled over the conclusion for months, until one morning in December 2012, after prayers at a prayer meeting.

1 THE ROOTING 1939

Resting my head on a shoulder, nestling my face, then moving side to side feeling and nestling, I searched and my eyes saw things, and I remember seeing things but I can't identify what I saw. I felt with my face turning side to side looking, and with all my attention focusing on my project, my passion of the moment which was soft dark hair, the very dark hair almost black, not brown, of my mother. I had just been there a minute ago, right near it. I remember the wrenching shock finding it gone, and the next memory was the rooting for the dark hair. I have only that baby memory of looking in vain for that hair, then weeping; and the memory of the comb or brush that the women all around gave me to stop me from crying. Along with that, I remember how tickled they were with me, smiling and laughing, then after that, wanting the brush and reaching for it, but in vain for that also suddenly was gone. Loss rooted there with me, warm in surrounding darkness, warm, comfortable and rooting, moving my head on the shoulder of the unknown woman who held me there. I must have resigned myself to the unknown woman and those around me who were large, beautiful, laughing and powerful, for I remember no more of that day.

A curtain is drawn across the window into the rest of that day and of those baby years until I was about two or three years old that I won't go into now. But I was told by Mom about a time at a Minnesota lake cottage, a get-together that I was taken to where all my mother's sisters gathered one time after I was born. It was before my mother left us, when she and the family once had left Michigan for her home back to Minnesota. I think it must have been one of those days that I remember. And I know, at that time, I was also told by Mom that they had to wean me from my Mother's breast because of her having to leave. She also told me there was a lot of family members there from both my Mother's and Father's side at the lake cottage, and one of my older cousin's husbands kept splashing water on my sister, making her cry so hard that it upset everyone.

I think of that periodically, and keep that memory in the back of my mind, wondering why and how it came to be remembered. I wonder now if something of that baby rooting on the unknown shoulder for dark hair is still there somewhere in the back of my mind? Did I search my whole life for that loss I felt? Was I rooting in the back of my mind into the unfathomable darkness of a forgotten and suppressed memory of childhood, for the lost dark hair of my mother? Had I been somehow calling, and drawing closer and closer to the answer, to the question and demanding, "I want her back?" I felt that loss of love deeply, more deeply than I ever knew. But someone else knew, and was waiting for me to ask the right person, the right question, to unlock the door to love. But that would take a long time, and in the meantime a lot happened.

It took a conversion and I have tried several times to write it down in order to get it straight and tell my story. In doing so, I started this conversion story four times. The first was in 1968, when I scribbled it in a black hard cover journal and there it remained until 2002. That was my first try but I did not get it all down or in any good order, and soon it was forgotten. Then in 2006, one cold day in February, I started it again. That failed because of depression and procrastination. I tried again later again in 2007 but left off writing without success. The last try was incomplete and waited in a file I named "Eyes Shut" in my computer documents.

Finally, in 2010, I started at it again, only more determined. I have to start with only part of that last try, and the old black journal, to refresh my memory. Generic and plain, it has held the story's pages quietly. I carried it with me as part of my "stuff" to several houses in the late sixties, and it even went to Alaska, in 1975 after my first divorce, to lay in various drawers and suitcases along many trails of adventure and loneliness. The book stayed closed through many tumultuous years; closed through those remaining in my first marriage and those of two other marriages ending in divorce. It was left mostly unopened as it traveled with me back home to Indiana after 15 years in Alaska. But in 2002, I opened it again and wrote a lot of the story and named it *Eyes Shut*. Well, that stayed in my computer and I opened it and worked on it a few times, but not until 2010 after I retired, did I give it a lot of thought and attempt to put it together in chronological order. I started writing a lot of it as chapters in my journal in the early mornings. Throughout the years, however, the gift that's inside the little journal book has never been forgotten, and I pray for enough faith, hope and strength to relate the story today. I am finally listening to that small quiet voice I have been aware of for years, finding that voice a gentle nudge to write. I pray for guidance as I write about the events of that December in 1967, long ago.

I wrote it down back then, telling myself it was so I would not forget it, though I doubt I ever will. Mostly I think I wrote it to arrange my thoughts chronologically and to include events and the environment surrounding all of it. It is like a puzzle with many pieces that fit together so beautifully; and, so beautiful is the faith that I have embraced I have longed to write about it, and tell every one about how I came to be Catholic.

2 ART'S GIRLS

I was born in 1939, the second daughter to my parents, Arthur and Edith who were first generation Norwegians. My Sister Ardis was two years older. Shortly after my birth, my mother became distraught and abusive to us girls. She could no longer care for us. My father had no recourse as she was violent, and finally when he had to have her put in jail, he decided to separate from her, taking custody of his daughters. We then moved away from our home on the farm and left the state. He first took us to his hometown and his mother, who already had raised 12 children plus two grandchildren. She pressed upon her oldest granddaughter Blanche to help, who at that time was married with no children just having given birth to a stillborn child; Blanche became my Mom; A few years ago she told me . "Ma said to me, Would you take Art's girls?" which she did. I was 7 months old when Mom "got" me and Ardis my sister. Then the combined family moved from Minnesota and Michigan to Indiana; my father and my uncle were searching for work and they landed jobs there. I will refer to my cousin as Mom in this narrative and to her husband Leo as Uncle and note that her husband was a devout Roman Catholic and that Ardis and I were both baptized in the Lutheran church in Minnesota. I grew up loving Mom deeply. I ask for God's blessing on these pages about my life and conversion. I pray also for perseverance to finish this work. I am thankful for renewed interest and strength given to me to write lately for the message in this story will never grow old.

After a couple of years, we moved to a very small town in Indiana in 1942, just after Pearl Harbor, because my uncle was drafted into the army. That is where the majority of my childhood was spent, with my father, sister, Mom, her husband, my uncle, and their two children born after he returned from the war in 1945. As small girls, my sister and I were sent to Sunday school every Sunday. We went just down the road to an actual little brown church in the town. I don't remember ever having a choice about it; I liked it and am thankful that my father saw to it that I went. This church-going was incorporated into our lives as part of the things to do and I learned what every little protestant child did and still does which is all the bible stories, important bible verses, and hymns for church and Sunday School. Sometimes we would stay for the adult worship service and listen to the sermon. Then, when my sister was thirteen and I was eleven, we both participated in the church choir and I just loved that. Many of the hymns are there in my mind for me to hum or sing yet to this day. The stories of Jesus and old testament prophets and heroes were well known by the time I was fourteen and quit attending that church.

In those years, I went to church camp every summer at Lake Syracuse and had a lot of fun there. At the end of the camping sessions there were always altar calls inviting everyone that wanted to accept Jesus into their hearts to walk forward to the altar. I did almost every time, not really understanding it at all. I remembering struggling with the thought that Jesus was in my heart already, wasn't he? And every time I went forward, I did not feel any different. So then one time, I remember standing and watching some others go forward and me not going because I went the year before, and nothing happened. I always tried to follow the teaching of Jesus told to me by the Sunday school teachers and could not see how a walk forward changed anything. But I kept trying and walking forward anyway just to be sure.

One time when I was about twelve years old my sister and I attended an evening service where an evangelist was to speak. I think that my dad did not know about this for he got upset later. My sister went forward to receive Jesus and I, not to lose out on that experience, followed her to the altar a few minutes later. The Sunday school teachers talked to us after that, and when they came to me, I guess I did not give the right answers because they went away saying I did not really understand. But I thought I did and they were wrong; What more was I supposed to do or know? Was there some big secret out there about Jesus that I was not privy to? Was there some way they could see into my heart to see Jesus there? Maybe He was not there. Would I ever be able to have Him there and know for sure? I think I thought that maybe they were right; He was not there and I would have to wait until some unknown time in the future.

I remember clearly the walk home that night when my sister said we should tell what we did by accepting Jesus, and how amazed I was, knowing that I was afraid to do so, not knowing why. Then, on arriving home, when she told dad he got very upset. I can't remember the words but remember his disgust. Now, I think he had a bad opinion about evangelists as I found out later on in life. I avoided saying anything to him; I didn't want him to yell at me.

One thing in particular I learned at that church was about "The Comforter". I heard about Him one day when the scripture was read in an adult service I attended. The preacher read a scripture and must have done some talking and explaining about the Comforter because I was terribly interested in that Comforter that Jesus promised to send to us. As far as I knew though, He seemed to be a secret seldom mentioned. Soon after that the church, which was named Evangelical United Brethren, joined with the Methodist church, a denomination that did not have regular altar calls or evangelists visiting. It then became United Methodist, a combination of the two previous names.

Picture of my sister and me in 1939

Me, Mom, Ardis, and Gail taken about the end of WW2.

My Father Art Erickson

3 CHURCHES

    ` My Uncle, Mom's husband, went every Sunday to his Catholic church and always referred to it as Mass. I just accepted that without question, as I did most things in those days. His daughter and son sometime went with him. Mom was Protestant and had not converted until later in her life, after I had my own conversion experience.

    I used to help my cousin memorize her catechism. In those days it was the old Baltimore Catechism. It seemed a strange thing unconnected to the stories I learned about in Sunday school. I learned of the fish with the coin inside, and the nets being empty of fish all day filling full of fish when Jesus spoke telling the disciples where to cast their nets. There were all the parables like the good Samaritan, how Jesus told of poor Lazarus, and my favorite, the story of Zachias who climbed a tree to see Jesus pass by, an all-time favorite to a tree climber like me!

But when I helped my cousin Gail, I remember always being amazed at the list of questions and answers she had to know and say verbatim for she was only five years old. I hadn't encountered anything of the like in my Sunday school down the road. I heard all the stories of Jesus and the fisherman Peter's empty net, of Lazarus raised from the dead, and Zachias who climbed the tree to see Jesus pass by. Nothing was demanded that I learn except that we all had to call back a reply from our seats to the question: "Why do we love Jesus?" Then our reply was to be, "Because He first loved us". Also we had to memorize John 3:16, and that was it for the hard part. The rest was bible stories, all pretty nice.

In the process of going over Gail's catechism with her so many times, however, I memorized the Hail Mary prayer. But I especially remember how I had to correct her and have her repeat it so many times; she was only five at the time and the project laid out before her I thought daunting. Then one evening, when I was especially frustrated during a study session in her room, it all came to a halt in a discussion. Gail imperiously informed me that **I was going to Hell**.

Now, I don't remember hell even being mentioned in Sunday school, but I must have had an idea about it, and that I did not ever want to end up there. She said that since I was not Catholic, I was going to Hell and that everyone who wasn't was going to hell too. I could not have been more amazed and shocked, as well as angry, at the accusation and I lit into her. I was at my wits end in defending myself against such a horrible accusation out of the blue without provocation, and with such finality. I began to cry because of the hateful denunciation of myself and my Sunday school and it became a screaming match. The grown-ups soon became aware and it ended up with me in tears being dragged out of the room by force. As I think back now I remember no one even tried to console me, and I don't remember anyone ever talking to me about hell at all, or even asking me why I was crying. I only remember as usual, I was supposed to stop crying, and it was a hard thing to do. The usual glass of water was given to me with the promise that it would help me quit crying, but it never did.

After that night, I was not allowed to help her any more. I resisted and tried and tried telling them it wouldn't happen again, but it made no difference. I was very disappointed about not helping her; it was special, I knew, and I enjoyed it. I also thought I might be pleasing Mom and my uncle by helping Gail. The whole argument had been resolved in the grown-up minds, and I forgot about it after a while, but I wonder now where it went in my mind, for I had not only been rejected by God but by them as well. I was soon to find out.

I was very surprised sometime later on Sunday morning, upon being awakened late for Sunday school, and found my sister was up already. I was still sleepy when I found out why I was awakened by my dad too late for church. I was appalled, because I had missed Sunday school at first, and then upset that I had forgotten about the day of Gail's first communion. and so I had attempted to get my clothes on and hurry to go with. When I was told not to get dressed because I couldn't go, I said I would hurry but no, they said, pictures had already been taken and they were leaving. Then I saw Gail on her way out the door in a beautiful white dress, and I noticed my sister right behind her in a brand new skirt with big beautiful flowers.

I was very hurt; my heart was broken. I felt so left out and alone that I started to weep. I remember my father tried to cheer me up and get me to stop crying, but I felt just torn inside and wept inconsolably. I could not stop the torrent of tears and pain. But he insisted that I stop crying and he insisted I go outside for a picture, saying he would take my picture so I could quit crying. He told me to hurry, to go out in my pajamas and not get dressed. I did as he said, following his instructions in my despair and hurried outside in my pajamas to stand for my picture too. And there I stood and can be seen in the snapshot he took standing there in my pajamas, and in the background Gail getting in the car and my sister in her big flowered skirt getting in after her. Did my dad plan that, I wonder?

What was he thinking? For many years later in 2004, when I was scanning those black and whites, I noticed the background and the memory was heavy and pregnant. I do not remember ever seeing that part of the picture until it showed up in the old black and white pictures found in my daughter's stuff after she died. The pajamas I noticed first, thinking how strange, and then after peering and seeing what was going on in the background the whole scene became clear. I can't find the one with them getting in the car in the background, but this was taken a few minutes earlier. In the one shown it looks like Gail is crying, she probably felt as bad as me and probably wanted me to go too. The picture puzzle seems solved now, but had my Father wanted me to remember? I don't know the answer to that one. And now sixty years later I remember about that skirt situation and it is also made clear. Now I know why she got a new skirt and I didn't. I had blocked it out not seeing her get in the car. But I remember that skirt and how I wanted one too, usually always getting new clothes at the same time as my sister. I had to wait a year or two because, I guess they were not in my size, and when I got a little older, one appeared for me one day only the flowers were a different color; it was still a little too long. But I have to laugh a little bit at myself about the skirt thing and show a picture of my sister and I some years later in the big flower skirts that went out of style by the time mine fit me. But I also know something else about the situation that some may feel far fetched but not for me. The incident lay deep, sleeping on the wet pillow of my childhood. It rested quietly and never disturbed me again along with the Hail Mary but they both came up again later on.   My Dad, my sister, and I continued to live with my uncle's family until us girls, "were old enough". Another reason things were to change, I know now, was because Mom's hands were full due to the effects Gail suffered from having polio when she was two years old. Gail was soon to be required to undergo three back surgeries to correct the crippling scoliosis she was left with that was only getting worse without surgery. This required her to be homebound in bed with almost total care from Mom during a span of about two years. I did not understand this back then though.

Growing up in those years was a lot different than now days. There was no television and although there were books to read there were only two in our household. *Heidi*, which my father read to us and *Maida's Little Shop*, which was Gail's book that I had to read for myself. And, I read both books several times I might add.

Besides going to Sunday School on Sundays and school down the road during the week, I climbed trees, ate green apples, hunted wild asparagus with my friend Meriem and rode my bike all over the little town. We had no television and I played with dolls until I was thirteen. Continuing on, this combined household continued until I was fourteen when my father took up his own household in a nearby town where my sister was in high school. Moving caused me feeling of rejection and leaving Mom was very traumatic and painful for me, so much so I can't describe it, but although the rejection I felt probably affected my life, it is not a major part of this story only a part of it pertains to my story and the main topic, which is my conversion experience.

My little cousin Michael was born in 1948

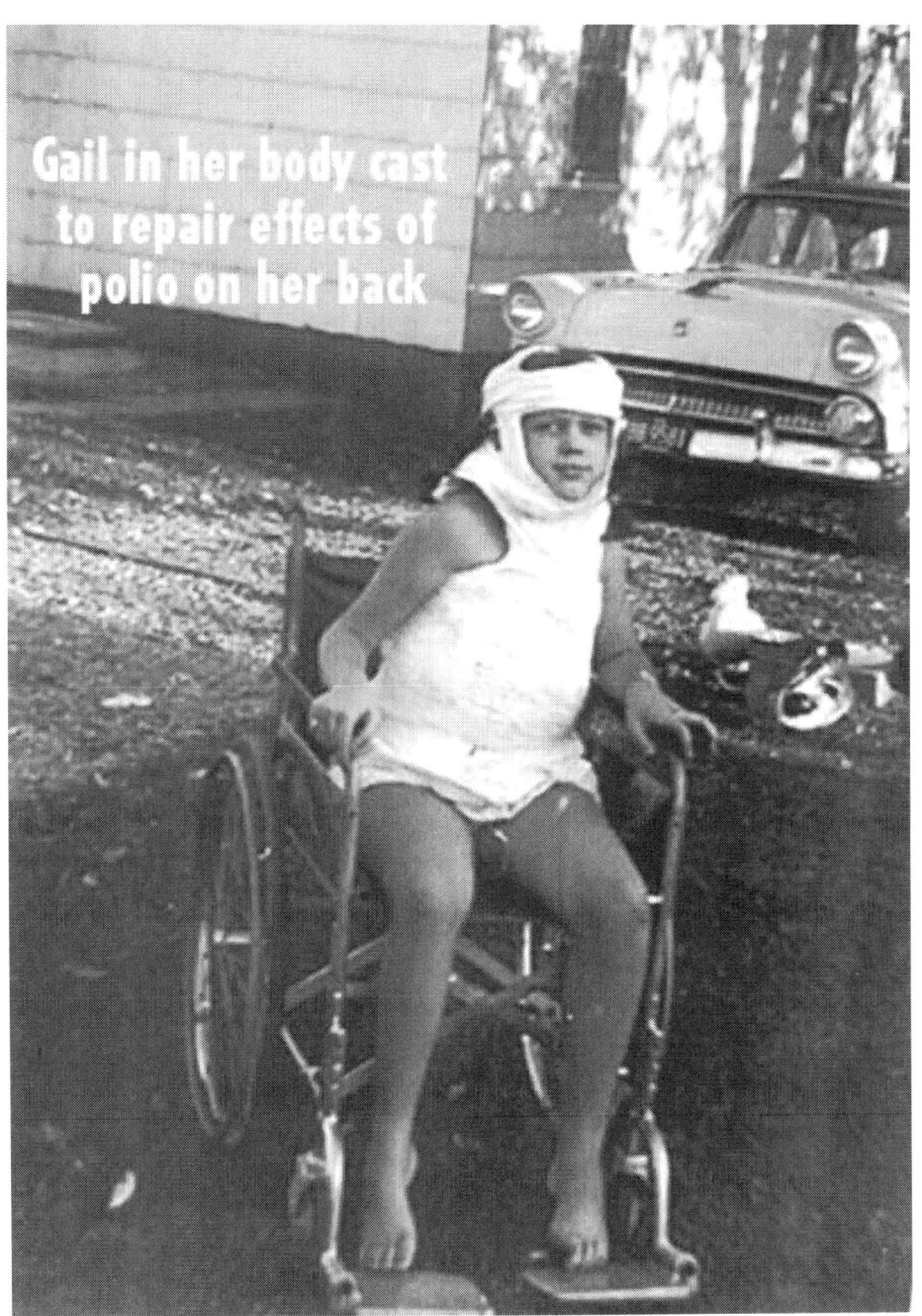

Gail in her body cast when she was 12

4 HIGH SCHOOL

Here I relate some things about my high school years after our move to the next town. When I started high school I did not attend church regularly. My sister had joined the EUB (Evangelical United Brethren) church after the revival service and she went back to the same church on most Sundays. I however, only attended the community nondenominational church periodically. I mainly concerned myself with school friends and books. I read avidly every book I could - because we lived across the street from the library. I read a variety of books, usually about seven every week. I read all the dog and horse stories that I could find, every Zane Grey written, some autobiographies, some religious books such as Martin Luther's, *Here I Stand*, and

Scholem Asch's *The Fisherman* and also *The Nazarene*. Recently, at a garage sale, I found one of several fantasy stories I read, referred to as the Graustark series by G.B. McCutcheon.

To fill in about those high school years, I need to add in this chapter an email I wrote in 2011 but never sent to Marilyn McMillan Bryant, my best friend in high school. I had put it aside, forgot to mail, it and then when I found it again it seemed too late to mail it. However it describes some things about my high school years and hints of my spiritual journey that I did not realize long ago.

"Dear Marilyn, Your questioning my church affiliation during our high school years caused me to put some things into writing. I had no formal church affiliation in those four high school years; however I did yearn in my heart for the Lord and attended the community church down the street a few times, and the Methodist church around the corner once. My sister Ardis would get up and drive her little Studebaker to the church that we attended weekly as young children, but I never went with her. She joined that church at fourteen years of age. But most Sundays I did not go to church. I always had my Bible handy though and did read it periodically. I prayed, as I remember, not infrequently. But back then I prayed mostly in relation to my emotional and psychological pains and concerns, wanting them to be taken care of by God I believe, desiring the Comforter.

My sister walked forward to receive Jesus one evening at a revival meeting held in the church basement before it changed to Methodist ways. I had gone also and followed her up to receive Jesus. However, they, (two grownups) decided that I was not a candidate for membership as they thought I did not understand what I was doing. And indeed maybe I did not. In fact I walked forward to altar calls before a few times at church camps and can't remember ever hearing an altar call where I did not want to go forward and receive Jesus in my heart. Indeed who would not want to receive Him? In retrospect though, I remember not understanding how going forward would accomplish receiving Jesus into my heart. It never seemed to. I also always went forward, concluding that if it was by golly, I was going to do it.

I never heard altar calls in church again until my Baptist days later in my life. I did not believe that I had received Jesus in my heart, and no one else believed I had either. It was never spoken of again anytime time after it happened. I was just dismissed back to my little girl ways wondering about Jesus, reading about Jesus, praying to Jesus, and believing he lived and said the things I read about but not ever coming into the knowledge of Him. I wanted it to be real I wanted it real.

Now, writing this down with you in mind, I see and understand that the Lord was there, but we do not always understand His ways as they are so far beyond our ways. Now thinking back to those teen years and how much or what I knew about the Lord, I cannot even begin to judge, as I am so far removed from the Sonja of that time. I do know that she was busy basking in all the friends the Lord had sent her. She had determined to pull herself out of the darkness, and depression of her later childhood. In other words, I just lived those high school years out very happily, enjoying school, friendships, activities, and lots of books from the library across the street. All of these things happily took up my high school years and I was so fortunate to have you and the other girls as my friends."

I continued on and closed the letter. Reading the letter now and searching back I found a window into my inner life hidden beneath the life happily shaped around me back then. It opened with some poignant memories and I find the memories of my friend's mothers more touching, more powerful, than all the basketball game dances, gossip sessions, beach outings, outdoor theaters, and books. And no one ever knew or could imagine such a thing. I could not either. They were passing moments, but, if even only snapshots in time, left indelible marks deep inside me. I wonder if those mothers ever knew or suspected my pain. Maybe they did but I didn't. However, mothers of my friends pose in windows deep inside into the teen me. They do this the same way that old black and white pictures point to me inside the little girl that's pictured in them. Mothers, Judy's, Norma's, Charmaine's, Sharon's, Joyce's, and Marilyn's, lean on window sills speaking softly.

    I remember them clearly, especially Charmaine's, unforgettable mother who always would take time to talk to me and sit down with me and discuss various thing that I can't remember now. What was important was her though and I can see that now. One other time frozen in my mind is one afternoon spent with Norma's mother who talked with me for over a couple of hours while I waited for Norma to wake up from a nap. How I loved and appreciated that talk with her! I know Judy's mother never knew how I marveled at her, or what I received when I tasted the bite of macaroni and cheese casserole Judy offered to me once. I had never seen or tasted anything like it, nor have I since. Although my father's cooking skills were far beyond most men's, he never made casseroles, pies, or other things that I thought belonged in the realm of women back then. There in my mind are Sharon's and Joyce's Sweet Mother's standing in their kitchens as I walk in their back door.

    I was and am nurtured somehow in just passing by and noticing their hands on the window sill. I catch a glimpse of some time, a conversation, or a word or two directed at me. And maybe of all things, I can smell the aroma of luscious, beautiful cookies coming with the wind over the window sill. Those very cookies that Judy's mother was baking one day that I only saw and could not stay and taste. Yes, the mothers of my friends were all wonderful and in a way, role models for me, though none were aware at the time, especially me.

And so, for the friendships of my high school years, I am forever grateful. There is another friend from my childhood Meriem, whose mother was the Girl Scout leader, always laughed a lot, and was so happy to be with us, take us places and teach us things. Meriem is my oldest friend and I cherish her friendship and memories of her mother, who was very good natured and always had a smile for me and laughed a lot.

I can see now that my friends were all a gift from God. He wanted me to play, to laugh, to enjoy wonderful company. I thank them, and I also thank God, for Mom, who did her best, and for all my friends' mothers, who didn't know they were doing anything at all. Remembering those year's my heart says, "Don't you know?" Yes, I know now Lord. I know - Thank You.

5 RONNIE

After High School I went to nurses training, having applied for and receiving a scholarship nearby Hospital's RN diploma program. There I dated a lot and a new world of nursing practice and medical books opened up before me. Along with that, we students were steady workers on duty at the hospital in the patient care units. I was really attracted to one certain guy during my third year there and became pregnant. His Name was Ronald and needless to say back in those days there were no special civil rights for a pregnant woman, I was dismissed with just three months left of the three year full-time diploma program that I had worked so hard for.

We were married in the local Roman Catholic Church close to where he lived and also near where Mom and my uncle lived. It was the same church that my uncle had belonged to ever since I was a child growing up in his house. Because my husband and his family were all Polish Catholics, I became aware that it was desired that I sign a paper to raise my children Catholic, and I had no problem with that at that time. That was my first encounter with a priest and it wasn't much more than a few questions and I signed the paper. In those years of my married life I stayed home and took care of my family and had four more children in the first six years of that marriage.

    I loved that time of my life. I cooked every meal for we did not have much money and never went out to eat. In those days the 1960's and 1970's, young families mainly ate at home. I have an idea that is not the norm for families these days. My husband went from job to job always having one though; sometimes he had up to three different jobs in one year. We always rented homes and moved often to a larger or different house. Times were hard and I had to budget carefully. One thing that was difficult and painful for me to deal with in our marriage was that my husband drank a lot. He drank mostly at bars after work, always staying late at the bars with his friends. His drinking increased with the years, and my frustration with his drinking grew also.

    In 1964 when I was pregnant with Arthur we moved to Gary, Indiana due to Ronnie taking a job there. It was about fifty miles from our home town and we lived there for over two years during which my younger son Arthur was born in October 1964.

    In 1966 when I was three months pregnant for Kim my youngest child, a neighbor lady invited me to go to her church revival one evening. I ended up joining that church which was of the Baptist variety just before we left Gary. And this happened to come about because of course, just as before when I was a child, I walked forward to receive Jesus. Only this time it was different; I was brought into the congregation and was baptized by immersion.

    A few months later, when I was eight months pregnant for

my daughter Kim, we moved back to Mishawaka due to my husband's job assignment. I continued going to a mission church there associated with the same Baptist church and even taught Sunday school. But still I had questions about the Holy Spirit and I questioned my friend one time and she had no answer for me. She only flipped it past her as if not relative to the faith of Jesus Christ's church. I was puzzled.

    My husbands drinking increased, and it seemed to make no difference to him if I was heartbroken or not. He never apologized once for his drinking, not for his behavior when coming home at 3 am, nor for any of his behavior when drunk. Because of his drinking habits I was constantly disappointed. He seldom came home for supper and never went to church, even when I asked him about it. I will mention that before I joined the Baptist church, I went to church by myself a few times a year to any protestant service near wherever we lived at the time. I almost always tried to go on Easter Sunday.

    My first husband Ronnie was not an entirely horrible person at all. On the contrary he was a happy go lucky guy. He made friends easily and was always ready with a smile and loved to make people laugh. He was the life of the party and maybe this was the downfall for our relationship and marriage; he could not refuse his friend's and co-worker's invitation to bars for drinks. I loved him and loved being with him but He would never come home after work and when at home on a weekend he would always find an excuse to leave. There were some other things involved in our break up too. I have included a picture of him taken in his late teens. He died when he was about 62 years old of a heart attack.

Ronnie

6 THE SNOOPY GOSPEL

So, it was in Gary that my spiritual journey began in earnest when my neighbor lady asked me to attend that revival meeting. It was mainly because I wanted my children to have some kind of religious education because so far they had had none at all, and my oldest was starting in the first grade. I started taking the kids to Sunday school right away. I was really happy that they were in Sunday school and I even enjoyed teaching the preschool class in the church after we moved back home from Gary.

The kids and I went to that Baptist church every Sunday. However, regardless of how I tried to have a normal life, it was becoming more and more difficult for me to cope with my husbands absences and drinking habit, especially in Gary where is seldom spent time at home. I grew lonely after we moved, for again for I was pregnant and with four small children, soon to have five children to take care of and had no help from him or even had his company for support. Also, in Gary, we were in a town about sixty miles from where we grew up and where our families lived and this added to my loneliness. But soon the job that my husband had came to an end when he found other employment back home and we packed up and moved back home a month before my giving birth to Kim. I was hopeful for better things to come, but something was changing.

I felt different about my church membership after I transferred to the new church even if it was of the same denomination. Even though I taught Sunday and all the kids went to Sunday school I was not settled in about the church. But after we had attended there a little over a year, a change in the way of those things began to take place. One day when I was waiting in a room of the church set off for office space to speak with the pastor, I perused some literature stacked up on a chair. The stack of pamphlets caught my eye so I read the literature while I waited, and found it to be quite anti-Catholic in nature. I was shocked and troubled by this because I did not learn about Christ in that way that brought such negativity and seemed to advocate animosity towards others of the Christian faith. I had never given the various denominations much thought before or even questioned it. But I had for the past year read my bible avidly and hungered in a way for more information about Christ and how to live a Christian life.

Then after that day I was beginning to question the entire system of different congregations and branches of congregations and denominations. This inner conflict was spurred on by the happenstance of the pamphlets that day; so they really started my spiritual search and study in depth. During this time, besides teaching a Sunday school class at church. I even went on a home visit to a neighboring town with the pastor and a friend of his. I did not know before time about the friend's accompanying us. At the time I remember being surprised, and a little uncomfortable, sitting in the back seat of the little Volkswagen behind the two men. And the visit seemed clumsy to me; the woman looked uncomfortable with our visit, and we did not stay long, nor did she end up even seeming to be interested in returning to the church that we represented.

I was not used to such home visits, though I was anxious to do things to please Jesus, and so I thought if this would do it, I was going to go along with it. I can't remember any of it except the few thing mentioned here, The car ride seemed long yet not much of it remembered at all and the reason for the long trip seemed flimsy. This seemed like weird church activity to me, and the pastor could do nothing but shake his head in consternation when I asked him about the woman we visited that day. Something about that trip did not add up in my mind, but I shrugged it off at the time.

One of my efforts to solve the inner conflict was to visit the local library, and so I began to collect every book about the many church doctrines I could find there to study. It seemed like a lot of churches, but the doctrines I found were all somewhat sketchy. I also thought it was puzzling and a terrible responsibility for one to have to decide upon which church, in that their eternal soul might be in danger if the wrong choice was made; something wasn't right!

At the same time my marriage was disintegrating. My husbands' drinking continued and with him closing the bars in the early mornings, and two jobs he was never home. We ended up with no time together, with no relationship, and with the burden of five children under seven years old being left to me alone. He refused to talk with me about it and also refused any of my overtures for a loving relationship and or conversation with my. I was a housekeeper, a cook and a washer of his clothes and it seemed that is all he wanted of me.

One time a few years into our marriage, I just left his clothes where he threw them for two weeks refusing to pick them up, and he just ignored me and the clothes until after several weeks, I could not stand the mess and relented. I did pick up and wash his clothes always after that, always no matter where he threw them, without complaint, somehow resigned to just loving him and not expecting much in return.

Introduced into this complicated situation was another element. I began to often feel no joy in any thing, nothing was of interest to me - no TV program that I used to watch caused me to even smile or have interest. It was as if I was not even there. Usual fiction books did not interest me. I only read my bible and other books about the Holy Spirit and Speaking in Tongues one of which was "The Gospel According To Snoopy". But, for the most part only the bible was in my hands, before my eyes, and my frustration grew as I poured over it daily, searching for the elusive Holy Spirit.

I remember I cooked and took care of the kids but the rest was just growing sadness with life holding no joy. But reading my bible every day satisfied some inner need, so I continued to study it, searching for answers to all my questions about faith, churches, salvation of souls, and most of all about the Holy Spirit, the comforter. My father stopped by daily as was his custom and I visited with him more than my always absent and or silent husband.

7 MYSTERIOUS

A few interesting and pivotal things happened that are factors in my conversion. One was the finding of the stack of pamphlets on a chair in something like an office room full of books and stacks of papers and books, or maybe it was one of the Sunday school class rooms. The pamphlet had encouraged all church members to evangelize the city where we lived and to be especially vigilant and hard working toward this goal because this was a Roman Catholic stronghold. That and the general theme of the writings made me feel uncomfortable. It was my first experience with anti-Catholicism. I couldn't see the point in that. And I was amazed, because I knew members of my family were Catholic and what was wrong with that. I realized I did not know what I had gotten into or anything about the Baptist church history or doctrine at all. As days went by into the autumn, my visits to the library continued but at the library I found out very little, only that many of the doctrines were bland and very much the same. There were only a few books about different churches and only one about doctrines of churches. Most of the descriptions were only a paragraph. But then again the doctrine lists of beliefs were short vague and many things I know now were not listed. If they were non-consequential and nothing was different about what they believed, then why were there all the divisions and different denominations? Then one cold day another interesting and pivotal thing happened near a corner outside the library. And this event was significant especially because the library was located less than a mile from my Baptist preacher's house.

    I mention it here because it belongs in this time sequence of events, but it's significance would not be understood until long after most of this the story is told. While I was backing out of the parking spot in the library parking lot and pulling out into the small road running beside it up to the main thoroughfare, I saw two men standing facing each other. It was a chilly autumn day and one of the men seemed younger, tall, lanky, poorly dressed with dirty baggy pants, and a hooded jacket that was long and greenish like an army thing of some kind. The hood of his jacket was up and over his bowed head almost obscuring his face. The other man with more of his face, his side view facing me was a tall, slightly heavier man, older, with a grey brimmed hat out of place except that it was cold outside, like my dad and other men wore in the 1940's. The brim was pulled forward and down to cover most of his forehead and his long grey trench coat hung low, almost to the ground. The coat's collar was pulled way up in a vain attempt to shield his chin and lower face.

    They hunched over a little, especially at least the older appearing one, who glanced towards me for an instance. Then just before I turned my head to pull away, I noticed their gloved hands held only waist high and sort of close to their bodies moved, and they each exchanged something with the other furtively. The image of these two men burned into my brain and grasped at my curiosity. I thought and thought about it afterwards and studied the memory seeking what it was about this that I needed to remember or even worry about. It bothered me somehow, and it did give me the creeps. The creeps though, I still remember to this day, did not cause any problem to me and for the most part I was blessed with being able to forget about it until the incident became one of noteworthy value which would become clear to me as time passed.

A few days after that, a further incident, an odd thing, happened on a night when my husband was away at his job out of town. I was always afraid at night in those years and would lay awake for a time trying to fall asleep, watchful and listening to every sound from the old house we rented on the south side of town.

But, the odd thing was that I woke up in the morning and remembered that I had been awakened in the middle of the night by an image of Jesus, a picture like the one in my husband's prayer book. I had found his old prayer book from his childhood one day and being curious about it had looked into and read parts of it once or twice in my search for more information about the comforter and various churches. At the same time that the image appeared before my eyes, I felt a spot on my breast become very warm and slightly penetrating like hot wax would feel if dropped on skin. Well, that was very strange but in the morning when I was dressing, I investigated the spot where I had felt the warmth and found a spot of wax. It was on my left side right over my heart and I simply scratched it off. It was very strange and so strange that I had hesitated to put this in the story until my daughter strongly encouraged me to do so, and not be afraid because it was part of what she called a puzzle in the story of my conversion. .

But one more time, something happened during one of the nights that my husband was on a job out of town. That night I was frightened, and watchful, trying to go to sleep, listening to every creaking sound from the old house as usual. When suddenly, I was awake and not sure what had awakened me. I stayed still and kept listening for a while then got up and peered down the stairs, afraid to check that out though by going down them. Before going back to bed, I checked the kid's room and they were sound asleep, so I went back to bed and laid listening, and listening. A few times I thought I heard something but passed it off to imagination and soon fell back to sleep. In the morning I was startled to be awakened by my husband coming in the bedroom. Then, when I went downstairs to make coffee, I started to wonder how he got in without waking me up because he did not have a key. I checked the door and it was unlocked. I asked him how he got in and he said the door was unlocked but I was sure I had locked and checked it due to my caution and fear.

I was the only one with a key but he insisted the door was open. I couldn't get over that fact because I was so sure I had locked the door. Then later that day, it started to warm up and the dining room got hot and stuffy. So I went to open the dining room's only window facing west towards two tree filled empty lots. It had two bushes outside of it, making that entire side of the house difficult to view from the well-lit intersection and road that bordered the lots. I found glass shattered just above the little lock between the two panes; its little half circle to secure it was in an unlocked position. Broken glass was all over the window top, sill, and on the floor. Oh no, I thought, someone must have broken in and left by unlocking and going out the back door. A little later I looked for my pretty little white comb that I always kept on the kitchen counter but could not find it anywhere. I looked for that comb for days but never found it. I had gotten it at a Tupper ware party and had managed to be able to hang onto it in a household where little children managed to help me lose many combs, brushes, and other small things. However, of all the strange things happening in my life during that time, a visit with the Baptist preacher was the most critical in bringing about a turn of events.

8 ENTER FIEND

The night when the preacher came to visit, my husband was home and since he was working out of town at the time it must have been a weekend night, probably a Friday. Now that I think back on that night maybe he was home because the preacher was coming over. I can't remember the reason for the preacher's visit, whether I called or if it was a regular pastoral visit or not, but I remember being anxious to talk with him, not telling anyone that I purported in my heart to find answers from him about some of the things I wondered about. So one of the first things I did was broach the subject of the Holy Spirit, and during preliminary talk went to get him some coffee in the kitchen where my husband was busy stirring something on the stove. He helped me get the coffee probably powdered instant coffee as a lot of people used it back then. After returning to my seat in the living room next to the preacher on the couch where we sat facing each other, I went further and told him about my old and persisting question, "What about the Holy Spirit?"

I only remember my question and the hunger for an answer. My desperate search for the Comforter that Jesus had promised was uppermost in my mind and I was determined to get an answer. I did not sense I had troubled him with the question only that he was strangely unable to respond to it. The answer he gave me wasn't satisfactory, so I pressed forward with some of the things I had been reading about. Why he was reluctant and evasive, I did not know, but I had hopes he could help me, having wondered about it far longer than anyone could imagine. The need had never left me, since the first time as a little girl in church, hearing the words of the passage in the bible, "Do not fear, neither be afraid. I will send the Comforter who will make all things known to you." And I knew what the word comfort meant. And I knew that I had not received any comfort ever and nothing that resembled it.

Well I continued and mentioned the book, "The Gospel According To Snoopy" then probed gently in the conversation for what he had to say about the Holy Spirit, the Comforter. And maybe he thought I questioned about the book itself, I don't know now. I only know my question and my hunger for the answer. The question was what of the "comforter" the Holy Spirit that believers were to be given. "Behold I will send the comforter." I had learned as a small girl. Those words still lay all alone inside me without any comfort. But I can remember when I questioned him, he said, "There are many voices out there," and he added "it is your choice which voice to listen to."

Well that was just about the end of it, and all he had to say to me. I was disappointed and puzzled with his seemingly avoidance of the subject of the Holy Spirit. He then set his coffee cup down, got up abruptly and walked away to take his leave. My husband Ron had been in the kitchen during our visit and he stepped into the doorway to the living room to see him through the door. While I wondered at the time, why Ronnie had excused himself into the kitchen back then, I now know it was because of his experience from his Catholic upbringing. That it was to be a visit between me and my pastor, and in Catholic circles those are special and private. Ronnie came in and stood waiting to bid him goodbye, but as the preacher took his ninth or tenth step and was halfway to the door he turned towards me with a farewell or some other statement that I have forgotten because: it was then I saw his face!

His face started to morph. Morph is a word I have since learned but it is entirely apt for this occurrence, because it best describes what happened. In an instant, fast yet like slow motion at once and yet at length, it turned into an ugly, vile, satanic visage that moved writhingly across his countenance moving, leering, and filled with hate. The visage had evil pouring forth from it like something alive. My eyes then flew to the top of the thing to see a writhing pyramid of snakes, twice as tall as his face, perched between two huge organ-like horns. It was a living headdress of revolting hideousness.

I was aghast, stunned, frozen in time! Somehow he left for I remember Ronnie seeing him out the door. I have no recollection of what response I had. Only that I realized Ron had been in the kitchen cooking something while he waited. Then the ordeal began as I realized in the aftermath of the horrible sight, that I was left with the ugly presence hanging on to me, touching me. It remained clinging to me. It constantly touched my skin. I could not make it go away. It just clung to me in its evilness. An evil way beyond any description tormented me. Believe me when I say evil, no evil, no multiple of evil, on earth is as great as the evil crawling forth from out of hell and searching the earth for the souls of men. There is no ugliness greater, dead or alive greater, than the live ugliness of the living image of Satan when you see him looking at you. There is nothing fouler, horrifying, repugnant, repulsive, dreadful, disgusting, unspeakable, appalling, horrid, vile, as the dread visage of Satan; and his breath coming near you. There is nothing like his leering glare, nothing so horrifying that brushes up against even your clothing, to touch you somehow, and leave his evil essence clinging to your skin.

    I desperately needed relief but just waited thinking it would go away but after a few days my skin still crawled. I was horrified and in a state of bewildered anxiety. I told my father and my husband about the evil thing touching my skin but they didn't know what to say and I can't remember now what they did say. I finally relented to my father's suggestion and went to the doctor now doubting my sanity for after all when I told Ronnie what I saw, I believe now he thought it a hallucination, and I am sure that my father thought the same thing. I went though in order to get some semblance of normality and a better feeling into my life. I was hoping that some medication would be the answer. The family doctor prescribed Tofranil one of the early anti-depressants, and said it was agitated depression and the bottle was filled to the brim with tiny pinkish pills and I did my best to take them as ordered.

9 MY SKIN CRAWLS

But after a couple weeks I reached a point when the pills made my legs rubbery and my gate wobbly so I quit taking them. They had not helped take away my skin crawling with the touch of evil. Everything still felt unreal. The treatment with the medical field was at a dead end, because after a few weeks for when I complained, more Tofranil of a higher dose was prescribed. It still was not helpful and only made things worse by causing me to run into things and have numb legs. Finally, for I really knew it was the devil that I had seen and something real of an evil nature and because of the horrible feeling on my skin of the evil touching it, I kept telling my husband about the devil. He was probably at the end of his rope and was inclined to half listen to me, "It was Satan!" I told my husband. And then I also told him that I needed to see a priest for an exorcism. I insisted that he make an appointment for me to see a priest. So he got an appointment with a priest at a local Catholic church near where we lived at the time.

When I got to the 7 pm appointment, my skin was yet crawling with the evil and I was terrified of telling about it again, I knew no one believed me. I was hopefully, dreadfully, completely in unchartered territory. The priest, very old, and dressed in black, heard me out without a word, sitting behind his desk, without an expression of anything that I could tell. After I had told him my story of events and what I saw and that I wondered about exorcisms, he simply told me that the church had no exorcism to do because they were not done anymore and so he could not offer me anything like that. I persisted in my need and tale and he finally asked me if I had read bible accounts of Jesus casting out devils and I said that I had. Then He pointed to the wall behind his chair saying, "Well, can you look at that cross back there?" He pointed to the crucifix on the wall behind him. I looked at the crucifix and then he also asked "Well you know Jesus delivered people from devils. and do you believe that?" I answered with, "yes, I do." then, that is all that I remember from that interview with that old priest. But, I can say this, as I walked out the door I was aware of something different in the evil presence that had clung to my skin so maliciously. It had fallen to the floor as I exited the room; the minute I crossed the threshold, I noticed this happen and I even looked down to see if I could see where it was. I could not see anything but knew it now lay, and hung around my feet like an evil, invisible cloud presence. There, it floated and swept around my feet and lower legs. It did not touch my skin any longer; my arms and body were completely free of it.

That was some relief but not enough to allow me freedom to live again. I still had to be rid of it. I could not go on in life with the thing there always following me, like invisible smoke around my feet and ankles, just a few inches from my skin. I went along with daily things, cooking for the kids, washing clothes, cleaning house, doing dishes, but was losing my mind with the evil thing always at me. I pleaded and prayed to God to help me. I prayed and prayed and read my bible but nothing made a difference. I still continued to see my doctor for help and was given increased doses of Tofranil but it was no use. It could not remove the evil thing hanging around my body. I only had reduced mental acuity and my legs felt like rubber. I had to quit taking it again as it made everything worse.

My doctor suggested that I admit myself into the hospital psychiatric ward to seek treatment and help. Finally, in a desperate measure, thinking I had nowhere else to turn, feeling futility and in defeat of my own recourses, in humiliation I admitted myself into the psych ward at the local hospital. I was afraid, for by then anything was preferable to the devil, and his constant evil presence touching me. I would go to any extreme to get rid of it, anything to have it leave me alone. I had no power of my own to be loosed of it, and was completely powerless, needed help, and willing to look everywhere without thought of pride or embarrassment of any kind. I hated myself, didn't understand what was happening to me, and was ashamed of my helplessness and apparent insanity. I had been searching and beseeching God in vain.

In the hospital those first minutes and hours are not recallable in my memory banks but I do know that one of the orderlies told me a few days later that he had never heard anyone cry out so loudly or scream in such torment and pain as I had done. He could not get over it.

For my part, I remember only my pain and sudden dark torment of a breaking, shattering heart, painful beyond description. I don't remember screaming out loud, only that there were my wretched inner cries that came from where they lived, deep down in my heart and soul. It was there where I reached with all my might and strength in desperation to cry for God to deliver me from the evil thing, that thing that groped about me. My terrified tormented heart screamed for relief from that thing that would not leave, that clung near to me, that haunted my body wherever I went. Its evil presence spoiled the air I breathed and even the very thoughts I spoke seemed dirtied with an evil indescribable in its horror. But my heart broke and shattered in pain and grief. It just broke!

10 FULL OF GRACE

With my heart breaking, and painfully tormented with I don't know what, I cried to Jesus, "Hear me, Jesus, please, hear me. Oh, hear me Jesus; help me Jesus." I cried, and wept over, and over in my soul with my heart torn into pieces, there seemed nothing I could do to be free of the torment I was in.

Then suddenly I was at once instantly, ushered, moved or transformed somehow to a place where I saw Jesus standing only a little ways off from me. There was Jesus, meek and mild in his white robe, in a humble place, a plateau of some kind. He was gazing in love, and with love flowing, to many people, throngs of people, writhing and reaching for him. They strained in anguish in a tremendous pit before Him. He just stood there, intent on them, waiting and focused completely. He only had eyes for them and no matter how I called out to him; He did not seem to hear me. I called and called, again and again, but to no avail. My heart broken in pieces in fearful torment I was afraid I was in hell already. The more I prayed and was rejected by Jesus the more painfully terrified I became. I felt like I was dangled over the great deep dark pit of hell.

Finally my eyes wandered over to the right side of Jesus and I saw Mary kneeling and facing the pit that was in front of her and toward my way; she seemed far away from me, like Jesus. She was on the edge of a great gulf or something similar that was between me and them. And I think now, I was on the opposite side of that pit or hanging over it I do not know if I was standing, sitting or floating. I only know I had been ushered to that level to see them both. I saw her kneeling with her hands folded in front of her as if in prayer.

The giant throngs of people over to the left in front of Jesus writhed, and swayed, straining with their arms lifted up high, reaching for him. Human souls all in torment, throngs of all kinds of people, grey; grey faces, clothed in grey, with horrible anguish filling their faces as they strove toward Jesus. Jesus, the pure, meek, shepherd watched them dressed in a white robe, gazing intently. He seemed to not hear me as He stood there before those souls in the pit, who cried without end, swaying and leaning towards him, their arms reaching high.

Suddenly I shifted my gaze to Mary, and with my eyes on Mary, I yearned towards her with thoughts of my children telling myself that she was a mother, maybe she would understand. And at the same time, I remembered the prayer I had taught Gail and I prayed the prayer I had helped my cousin memorize many years before. With motherhood the only thing that caused me to speak, I lifted my prayer. With the Hail Mary on my lips, but really tearing out of my broken heart, I had to dare to ask her help. I was desperate to do anything and I could hold nothing back to reach Jesus, who I believed was the only one who was able to free me from the devil that had such a hold on my being. I prayed with all my heart just that one Hail Mary, with all my heart, groping and straining inside for help to reach Jesus for release from the evil thing, and for the Comforter spoken of in the Bible, the gift of the Spirit bestowed on believers.

I had searched in my heart when I saw Mary and thought, I was a mother, Mary was a mother, "Maybe Mary", and turned to her and prayed. "Hail Mary, full of grace, the Lord is with you. Blessed are you among women and blessed is the fruit of your womb, Jesus. Holy Mary, Mother of God, pray for us sinners now and at the hour of our death. Amen." Along with my words my soul cried out to her with the request of my burning heart, my heart broken and in torment of unknown depth, spoke my heart words to her and they were immediately transmitted to her son and within the same instant it seemed she looked at me, then turned to Him. He turned ever so instantly to me, that there was nothing in the instant of time that could be measured, and I was swept away somehow and healed.

11 STILLED AND BEHELD

Now, I feel compelled to repeat again that the whole sequence of events in that place, from the time I was ushered in until I lay on the bed was instantaneous;   It was as if in one instance all things took place when I prayed the Hail Mary. My torment and calling out, being ushered in to where I saw Jesus and Mary, the sights, the pit, the heaving throngs of grey souls, seeing Jesus, praying to Jesus, Him not hearing me, seeing Mary, thinking motherhood, thought of asking help from Mary, the hail Mary, the look from her to me, then to Jesus, then from Jesus, to me, healing me with the look itself, being released and swept away, all in one instance, yet in order. I was released; the evil had been taken away and it was completely gone.
      Suddenly I was aware of the room I was in, and the experience reverberated in my whole being as I lay there, my heart

taking on newness and filling to the brim, overflowing with love, indescribable love. Love was pouring into my heart and soul and I was given a new heart.

Love unimaginably intense and wonderful had been poured into my heart. With the love pouring, words also flowed at the same time. And words came emitting out of my new heart, came flowing in and out in the same instance. The emission of words flowed out of my soul to my understanding were very clear and deep, "If your heart does not condemn you, neither do I." Now, these words were intensely pure words and at the same time not only words but purely translated to me in the form of understanding and with sound of words in my heart. They were softly, clearly, even visible to the eye of my heart, emitting out of the deep there, like ticker tape of flowing words. It was love; it was truth; it was word translated to me, for my understanding, to grasp it there inside first.

The instantaneous turning of Jesus to his mother, His humbleness, her obedience, and humility, were of the utmost from the appearance that came to my inner eye. This all appeared even the beholding them, as if through my body's eyes. I beheld them, Jesus and Mary, as humble earthly human beings. My asking was not really spoken, only just an "asking." It was as if "asking" could be a title describing a thing. I only now can know it was my need emitted to them, with and in prayer.

After the words from out and within my heart, I rested in wonder for a time, then I realized a presence near me in the room that had transmitted its presence to me. I felt the love from the being and Love's presence in the being there in the room.

Slowly I beheld Him. I knew then God's gloriousness and all encompassing love that was something like a living, moving, breathing cloud of love. He had made himself present to me and I was stilled; my whole being was stilled. for how long I do not know. Then, in my soul I sensed a change and discerned He was taking leave and I did not want Him to leave me, I longed after Him yet was so full of the spirit of love He had given me.

Then I remembered something and I reached with my being to bring Him back for the question, one remnant of my quest that I had struggled with so mightily before this happening. I asked the Holy Presence this thought, what about the right church? Is there a right church? What was the church to turn to, the way to worship Him, which church? What about the answer to the thing I had searched out for in every book I could find on the subject. For, I had sought an answer, pouring over the scriptures daily for so long a time. I had been going in what I like to call spiraling, to the end of my thought processes, to find an answer. God immediately so gently and kindly responded to me then, filtering understanding into my soul as an answer.

His words are truly not like ours. They are truly refined, truly pure, distilled down to the essence of truth and knowledge itself. They are living and were gently dropped into me and an ingredient in His words to me this time was his chiding. It was so lovely and gentle I could live on and in it forever. The presence did not hesitate to tell me, did not slow in any way the allowing of this to flow into my mind's understanding: The chiding was this. *"You ask?"* Then, I received, *"Do you not know?"* meaning, should not I already understand that all prayers of a man belong to God? It was like He said *"Prayers, they come in unto me, are owned by, and are my possession and business."* They are HIS. And then I asked with or saw a picture and I remember the picture and answers were one and the same. I remember picturing men in prayer even a Muslim and maybe others of all kinds. *"Yes,"* came the understanding to me. *"All prayers to me are mine and belong to me."*

The answer was blessed for me, and filled me with unimaginable understanding, love and kindness. It was kind and gentle. It was delivered by the Father to His bewildered child, me, without even sadness, only love, pure love. I cherish the chiding, the answer, the healing, the words, the Father, the Son, The Spirit, and Mary. It was all one supernatural event, and an indelible experience. In addition He corrected me so gently I have never forgotten. And I knew inside me the Holy spirit.

I no longer question God, although I have made many mistakes since then. I do wonder about things though, but mainly I pray about things, I rail, I weep, I groan in the spirit. But, at all times I know His love. He loves me who am most unworthy of his love. No way could I ever do anything to deserve the immense love he holds in store. I hardly dare even speak of my own unworthiness because worthiness is his business. I cannot ever make myself worthy. No one can.

Not mine, not my business is another man's prayers. How can I look at another's prayers that he offers and sends to God and judge it. It is God's to look at and see and feel and answer. "How could I not know this?" That seemed to be the question I should ask myself. I had never looked at my quest for an answer in that way. It did not occur to me that in a way I might be saying one was right and discarding or judging the other lesser or wrong. I felt like I was walking on a cloud. That was another element of the after math I felt sometimes like I floated and time did not seem to move like it always has. It was slower, and I seemed sometimes to float slowly up and down the hallway in the hospital. That sensation slowly wore off and I went home from the hospital two weeks after Christmas.

12 A SECOND ENCOUNTER

    Someone prayed for me, which was my constant thought when wondering what brought my plight to the attention of God. Sometimes I would wonder who could have prayed for me and in my ignorance I didn't realize what was right before me. You see I did not know a lot about Mary or God and His ways either. I thought I had appealed to Him for so long, and so hard, without success, that someone else on earth had to ask Him to heal me. I wondered if it was my uncle or a priest or someone like that. Now, of course I know who it was, it was Mary, who had prayed to her son in that instant, and it was me who had put in the request desperately to her and she heard me. Even though I know she turned to him and gained my healing I thought myself not worthy to be heard somehow, who could ever figure out why.

I also had other thoughts about forgiveness that were a mystery to me. Forgiveness for my sins had occurred I realized for I felt washed clean and free of any condemnation as the word said, free from any blame from myself or from God. This was to such a great and immense extent that it seemed to cover all my sins of any degree or kind possible, if the amount of forgiveness matched the amount of sin. This might sound terrible, but I wondered, had I sinned that much that I should be forgiven to such an immense degree of love? The forgiveness feeling of love seemed to fill up a vast gulf of time as if to cover all my past sins committed and any that I might commit in the future. It was like I could not even sin, like I was not ever to be condemned, and like I was removed from this world of sin, and all was good.

I felt loved beyond my imagination but at the same time I knew I would sin again because all are sinners on the earth. The greatness of the love poured inside my soul was so overwhelming that my mind tottered, and reeled with trying to comprehend it.

There was no one I knew who would understand, and I told no one at first, for after all it was important that I get out of the hospital fast because I was rid of the devil. So, I did not want to add this incredible event to what the doctor had to consider in my discharge plans, thus I was careful as to how much I said about what caused my relief of the torment.

I did tell my husband and others when I got home, but all of their responses were mostly muted. It was like they did not know what to say to me and so said nothing. I also had neither read nor heard of any modern day events like this or any thing similar so, I did not have any reference, other than certain Bible verses to relate this healing event in my life. Still, I knew without a doubt it was God given and that the love in my heart was a gift that was indelible.

Still floating a little at times, one day after coming home from the hospital, I laid down on the couch with my youngest daughter Kim in my arms. The three oldest were in school and my younger son, Art who was three years old, was still asleep. I cuddled there with my baby thinking and remembering again my time with God the week before Christmas. I held her tight to me and felt so full of God's love in my heart that I had a wild thought, maybe if I held her there, some of God's love would go into her if I prayed. I wanted my baby also to know this intense wholeness, this sense of being loved, that inhabited the new heart given to me. So I started to think that and hope and pray that, pressing her close to me.

Something happened for the next thing I remember I was standing before God. He was in the opening in the room somehow in a swirling living circle again and His being was love itself. He lived and breathed love and happiness unfathomable, unspeakable. This love flowed out from him and inhabited me and it seemed all the air in the room or the part I was aware of. For, I could only behold Him the trinity and I seemed to only stand beholding Him and being beheld by Him. I was looked into deeply.

I don't know the beginning or the start or the becoming of this opening. It was like the sky opened, rather, a void split into the air in the room. The air in the room must have spread before me and time too filled with something wonderfully beautiful and unspeakably loving. This somehow transparent window into another world was a lens, but somehow before me filled with a holy, very holy, swirling, moving, living, breathing, essence of a beautiful, vibrant, being of pure love.

I peered with an eye given to me in my being somehow, and stood beholding and being beheld, transfixed. But my soul cannot translate to my understanding all Love's immensity in this being. It's just known, offered somehow to an eye and a heart to behold, but not really ever explainable. We spoke somehow, communication coming somehow instantly to my heart, for who I beheld was heart, presence, being, love indescribable. I remember suddenly realizing I wanted to go be with Him and into him and become His completely and alone his. So strong was this longing that I could hardly bear it. I wanted to be with him, like right in him, entirely swallowed up by him, belonging to Him. I wanted to serve him too totally and deeply. I remember next thinking that I could not go, could not leave to be with Him, because I had five children to raise.

Tony, Linda, Art, Ann, and Kim is in front,
The 4 youngest were baptized in 1968

13 WHEN KIM IS 21

I was suddenly confused with my contradicting feelings and felt pulled in half with my longing for this love, this God being who beheld me, and owned me entirely, heart, and soul, and then my children's needs. How was I to serve God? I wanted to go there to be with Him? To do so totally on earth I thought surely I had to be a nun or what or how? And then, what about my children, who would take care of them? Since I had been raised without my mother, I knew it was important for me to stay and continue mothering them. Since I realized during the whole conversation with myself, that in order to really be with God the way I longed to be, I would have to die, so an additional thought was suicide, which I discarded immediately knowing suicide was out of the question. What was I to do?

I turned to God in my mind or body or heart, I do not know only that I communicated to him how much I wanted to be with Him and love him and serve him. But, since I could not die and be with him, I would have to stay and raise my children. Then the thought came that I would serve Him when my daughter was of age. I would serve him completely when my youngest Kim was twenty-one years old. And I thought I communicated that to Him. Now years later I realize God knew before me what all my thoughts, fears and concerns were and His answers just flowed into my consciousness at the same time as I thought them.

When Kim was twenty one would be when I would be really serving him. Suddenly, that strangely and calmly settled the contradictory feelings that pulled at my heart. It seemed these were my thoughts to Him, but now all these years later I wonder if they were not planted by Him, into me, as now I think he told me when I would finally serve him completely. I could not have thought any thought in the state I was in. I say this because of knowing how my life turned corners and went upside down after that and I was drawn so far away from who I was that day, that who could recognize who I had become. And those words, "when my youngest daughter is twenty one" come to haunt me to this day.

Right after the final communication, God's presence began to take his leave and I was distraught not wanting to lose Him, but knowing I had to turn and go to my children.

I became aware of Kim who was standing by one of the kitchen cupboards where I kept pots and pans, as He faded, and melted out of the room, His presence withdrawing gently out of the very molecules of the air. Somehow I was made to be aware, and to behold Him leave, and see His swirling amorphous cloudlike loving presence go slipping and fading softly away. I mourned inside but turned and suddenly was aware of the grey darkness of the room without Him; because of the sudden loss of his lovely, indescribable presence of light; everything was stark and grey-like in comparison to being in the light of His presence.

The whole room and every piece of air and light in it was dimmer than I remembered it, and I knew I would have to sin again because of the despairing stuff of life, raising children, making mistakes, white lies, and choosing the wrong things. I felt I would become dirty and grey and dimmed like the room with sin. I was very aware at first of the dimmer light, and greyness of the room in comparison to standing in the Presence, but soon it faded and all seemed a normal light like I was familiar with.

A few days after that I stopped taking the bright, blue, pretty pills they sent home with me. I felt generally calm, had no strange sights of anything, and went about my daily work around the house and taking care of the kids pretty joyfully compared to how I was before. I no longer felt the extreme need to devour every word in the bible, for deep in my heart was the peace of the Comforter I had been searching for. I had been filled with His peace by the One who had the answers to everything. The awareness of my sinning disappeared, but a few years later I sure sinned, and when I look back at my life in those years, I am amazed at all that transpired.

After I was home a few weeks, I pressed upon my husband to get me an appointment with the same priest to take instructions to join the Catholic church. He did, and I went to my first appointment, though much to my disappointment we never touched any thing pertinent in the study Catholicism, nor information about how I could become Catholic. I had no reference by which to judge a session for admittance to the church, but we only rehashed my visions and happenings and such, I told him how I was healed, and he was carefully, non responsive in any manner. I can't remember all that I told him, but I remember knowing he did not believe me, or even say anything nice to me about it when I told him I was healed. He was a little stand offish, probably not used to hearing anyone say they saw the virgin Mary and Jesus, and claiming a healing. Now looking back on it after all the reading and studying of the Catholic faith and mystics of the past centuries, I am amazed no one told me about them when I told them my story. I had no idea any one had ever had an experience as I had had; I had no idea anyone had seen purgatory or hell, or had been transported to ecstasy.

To be honest, I left there confused because he did not believe me, and wondered if that was going to be a problem. At any rate I did not have to worry because the next week I found out from my husband, that found out from his mother, that my appointment was cancelled and of all things, it was because the priest had died of a heart attack. So for whatever reason, I put off thoughts to join the Catholic church during that time. I felt stopped in my tracks, an odd-ball. My faith in God never changed, only the attention I gave to him. However I did go to Mass and all the kids were baptized a few months later and were subsequently raised Catholic.

My husband's inattentiveness, drinking and slipping off every chance he got continued. It was of no use for me to address my unhappiness with his behavior, and there was no way for me to get through to him about my pain and loneliness; he refused to talk about it and would "clam up", leaving me with intense frustration and filled with futility, to the extent that one morning, after a particular long bout of drinking, I told him to leave, and he without a word to me, got up, took some clothes, and left without any further adieu. He did not come back, did not call even once to resolve the issue, or say he would try to change his drinking habits. We were divorced a year later and I was then a single mother of five children.

14 THE AFTERMATH

      I still continued to go to the Catholic church but never joined, and so never went to communion. But, my children were all catechized in the Catholic church up to first communion and an early confirmation some in the time before my divorce and some in those days after the divorce.

      I was devastated by the divorce and very lonely. About a year or so later I met an old acquaintance, Tom. We dated and then ended up getting married. His three children came to live with us so we became a family of ten. I stayed at home and cooked, and took care of the house, and kids. I loved it but soon Tom found a new job up north in Alaska where he had been before. It wasn't long before we left for Alaska with our family but only with one of his children, as the two youngest chose to stay and live with their mother.

It was in 1975 when we left for Alaska with our combined families for him to work on the Alaska oil pipeline. The trip going up the Alcan in those years was arduous and longer that it is now. The road through the mountainous regions of Canada and Alaska was completely gravel and barely two-way in some spots. It was quite an adventure for all of us but we soon got used to another way of life. In Alaska things are different but it is hard to explain how. There are some things about life, your job, what you wear, and what you say that are not important there, and are more so here. I missed those hard to define things when I left, replacing them with malls, thousands of roads, stores, and recreational activities. It was a culture shock coming back home. But I also gained being closer to my family and a variety of other needful things that add to a full life too. Still I find that I love winter and enjoy the quiet and solitude and slowing down of life activities that takes place when it snows.

I lived there for fifteen years but Tom about thirteen. The time in Alaska was colorful and eventful. Tom was reachable and loving for about the first five years and our life was full. But then everything was different there, so it seems my church relationships changed too. I don't know why but my church going became less regular, and dropped drastically for a few years.

I have added a picture of the kids on the next page. This picture was taken in 1975 when we just arrived in Fairbanks at mile zero of the Alcan. From left to right you see Tommy Jr. Arthur, Tony my son in back, the youngest Kim in front, Linda my oldest daughter and Ann Marie who now lives in California, I'm behind her. There was an information and tourist attraction cabin near where the sign was displayed.

On arriving in Alaska

Then, after about five or six years, Tom's drinking became a problem too, and I wanted to fix it. So, I started going to Alanon after being advised by a priest, who sent me to a woman, who was in Alanon and also a charismatic catholic prayer group. Tom worked a steady job up north six weeks at a time on the pipeline and was gone all the time, and then he went to California, to work for a year there. Our communication just dwindled and stopped until I realized the relationship did not exist, and I was living without a husband again.

I had started going to mass again in Fairbanks frequently during those troubled times in my marriage to Tom, and our marriage grew more difficult to be even realized as a marriage because of his absence. I went to the priest of the church I attended for counseling about the problems in our marriage and he sent me to someone in the parish who he thought could help me. a woman named Ruth. That is how I met Ruth and became friends with her. She took me to my first Alanon meeting and that began my education about alcoholism. I began to attend the meetings regularly and I learned a lot. My knowledge base about how to cope with alcoholism and everything about it grew. The support Alanon groups provided was of immeasurable help also. My life became more manageable because of Mass and Alanon. Then Ruth also found out about my interest in her charismatic prayer group and soon I was taken to my first prayer meeting. Ruth became the first personal friend that I had made in Fairbanks, my other friends being those that I worked with, and one other that I had met through my oldest daughter Linda.

The charismatic prayer meeting before long, became a bright spot in my life. I loved the songs, the people there, the Bible study, the sharing and praising God; it felt so right and I just loved it. This was a dream come true; something I had been wanting ever since first reading the "Gospel According to Snoopy". At last I was where there were people who knew of the Holy Spirit and could speak of Him. Soon, I myself was baptized into the fullness of the spirit too. I loved those prayer meetings and all the friends I made there; they are special people I will never forget. I also became employed at the Pioneer Home, which was a job I finally enjoyed and did well at. I worked there for six and a half years. I felt more at home than I had in many years since as a young child; things were beginning to go very well. I didn't know it at first but the prayer meetings were the beginning of new and better things in my life. but it took a while for me to see it.

After my husband, Tom, had been absent for a year working in California, he came home, He just had never been at home for a long time, either working up north in Prudhoe Bay or out of town, and his son had moved out to live with a friend. The dissolution of our marriage was inevitable, and he was seeing someone else, so I sued for a divorce.

Single again, I went back to work, and I continued going to Mass, Alanon, and prayer meetings. My three oldest children had all grown up moved out of the house.

Soon, after those two last years of married life but living alone, and another year or so after the divorce alone, I became lonely and in spite of my Alanon enlightenment, married another man who drank. With each alcoholic I was attracted to, their disease was more damaging to them than the last, and so was our relationship, just as I had learned in Alanon. To put it in a nutshell I will say the few years in which I met and married my third husband who also worked up north periodically and drank were just five lost years in which I wavered back and forth from going to Mass and not going. While married to him my hours off work were spent roaming the bars on second street with him, drinking coffee while he drank beer, and listening to bar talk. He was a brilliant and interesting person who paid more attention to me than my previous husbands but was also very verbally abusive. He seemed to need me, and I thought I could help him, like most women who continue to marry abusive alcoholics. time, and time again. Who knows where my mind was. I just only wanted a husband, thought I needed one, that was all, but that was not to be. I did take two year's of college courses in those years in Art, drawing, chemistry and writing, and fell in love with writing, when keeping a journal was required for English 101. I also picked up the wonderful habit of listening to audio book tapes to get to sleep. But following my husband around became like an obsession or a bad habit that took up most of my life off work, and my mass and prayer group attendance began failing. Two years into the marriage it became quickly rocky, and also my father passed away, so I made a trip back home which made me homesick and sad.

During this relationship The two youngest of my children had left home, I had terrible worries for them and life was getting hectic and confused. So because of that, the verbal abuse, and because I simply could not afford to support his drinking, I decided to call it quits with the third marriage, and it was dissolved. After that my life changed; I had a different inner peace, resolve and respect for myself and life. My entire life took on a new dimension somehow, and I felt in some way cured, and never again have I felt the need to look for a husband.

But any reprieve from traumatic events was not in store for me, because sudden disaster fell. and it concerned my youngest daughter Kim.

15 KIM

Kim was killed in an Automobile accident July 10th 1988. I go back a little bit here. My daughter Kim had a troubled life in her teens and my single parenting skills weakened while working to pay bills. At about 17 years old she opted to live with one of her girl friends family, and then shortly after that moved in with her boyfriend; subsequently she became pregnant and had a baby boy she named James, born in October 1985 a week after her 19th birthday, my first grandchild. I was so happy to have a grandchild, although she was young, I hoped for the best and she was on her way to getting her life in order.

I am not relating Kim's story entirely because it is so precious and sad. But I will say a few things. I believe that legalizing Marijuana as it is legalized in Alaska is detrimental to every child where it exists. I know because in those years and maybe yet today, drugs and alcohol ruled teen lives in Fairbanks, and greatly contributed to the problems in my children's life; it figured drastically and in the end sadly in Kim's. My life was turned upside down with her sudden death in an automobile accident, and it has never been the same since.

    I was devastated to say the least for there is no way anyone can describe how it feels to lose a child. Only those who have gone through it can understand; it was awful. Instead, I will relate that Kim was brave beyond whatever I could be, and I once saw her showing more compassion to one of the old patients in the Pioneer Home, where I worked than I ever thought I did in my entire life of nursing. She was turning her life around and quit doing drugs. She had a part time job monitoring and walking for the evening hours with an old gentleman who had Alzheimer's disease needing an attendant for constant surveillance during most waking hours due to his uninhibited behavior traits. She talked with him and walked with him around the nursing home halls.

    One night after he had been put to bed by us she walked past his room to peek in and see if he was sleeping but yelled out in alarm, putting his call light on. As he sometimes did. he had gotten out of bed on his long thin weakened legs, and fallen to the hard floor. My co-worker and I went right away to answer the light and alarming call, finding Kim on the floor kneeling beside a small pool of blood, holding the man's head in her lap. She was weeping and gazing down at him. She looked down on him with such pity that when looking up at me and saying "oh Mom". The compassion in her voice, and face was like I had never seen before.

    In fact, her compassion struck deep in my heart to help me define it, and I never forgot it; for since that day I use it as a guide to search it out and hopefully find even a little of it in my life. It's my injured heart that now needs the constant monitoring. She was a kind, beautiful, child, recklessly lost, but brave and died because of it. After her death, I was in constant turmoil, searching week after week for her killer in every way I could think of, and in the end finally letting go of it, knowing I may never know the truth of what happened, or why. I now know it's not the most important thing here on earth to know the truth of what happened. I still continued with my employment at the pioneer home trying to hold the pieces of my life together, and get it on a better path than what I had wandered into.

    I received great consolation from the priest at the church and the prayer group. I had no extended family in Fairbanks to gather around and help with the funeral details. Kim's viewing and rosary service the night before her funeral was packed with people and standing room only in back. The next day was the funeral mass of resurrection for her offered at Immaculate Conception Catholic church downtown Fairbanks, and it overflowed with people; there were so many people the church could not hold them all. The mass was so moving that I will never forget the young priest there and when he lifted up the host after consecration. I have included a poem here that I wrote about the mass. Right after the mass on the steps of the church, I spoke with the priest about becoming Catholic.

<u>Priest Eyes</u>
Oh the candles, the people, oh the choir and the casket,
Oh the images that crowd my mind like unwilling
And unwelcome guests in my consciousness.
Oh that I should hear prayers, see the burning eyes of the priest.
Oh that I should ever even see all that was there before me.
The table is set, oh that I should feel, oh the hot tears that well.
Pushing behind my face for there before me, what did I see?
The table, the candles, the casket, the pews, oh that I should see
Only the burning eyes of the priest, drew me back, drew me on.
What burned there that I should see was no small spark,
was not new, was not old, was not consuming, yet consumed.
Did you know of the fire in your eyes, glowing ember eyes priest.

In October of 1988 in Fairbanks, just before my daughter would have turned twenty two, I entered RCIA class, which is the Rite of Christian Initiation of Adults, in the Catholic Church. I was confirmed and had my first communion on March 25th 1989. Afterwards, I frequently attended daily mass and my prayer life deepened with receiving the Eucharist and attending weekly prayer meetings. I started learning about God, more about Him than I ever thought possible and He lived in my life in a new way. Through listening and writing in my journal daily I discovered that I felt especially close to him at times when I would be in a muse or in deep thought about a subject. The Comforter was abiding.

My whole life changed when becoming Catholic and I realize now, inexplicably, that the events happening after my entrance into the Catholic Church drastically figured into everything fortuitous and good in life, my plans, and their outcome. Even the long trip driving out of Alaska to the lower forty eight seemed to go like clockwork. Good things, like stability and inner peace seemed to have entered into my life things that I had not known before. I was not to realize at first though how much, and also how deeply, events tied into the events of December 1967. Although, once shortly after her death having coffee at my regular coffee house and thinking about Kim, I had sadly noted and reflected on how in the communication with the Lord back then had been so prophetic and I was mortified, and suddenly in wonder how she had been twenty one when she died. I left Alaska on her birthday, the nineteenth of October, drove myself out and down the Alcan bound for home. How striking the date, I muse about it now. The date was not planned other than it was after my last paycheck.

Some of what happened the first three years when I got back home is covered in my book, "Something Lovingly Planned". I had written the name of the book that fits this occurrence in an October journal entry written just before leaving Alaska. Many times I have found my journal to record prayers, requests or word that show up in my life later. As I first scribble my thoughts down and then sometime later type it up and find out what I really did say on a particular day in the past.

This lovely picture taken two weeks before my daughter Kim died shows her at 21, smiling on the left while Linda, her older sister smiles back.

16 OCTOBER

It was a cold, windy day in Fairbanks when I wrote the following journal entry, while sitting in a restaurant on the corner of Cushman Street and Airport Way.

<u>October 3, 1989 entry</u>

What do you want of me now Lord
Now that October is here?
Bringing crisp, colder mornings,
Cold, cold, as the finger of fear,
Which tries to slip into my cheer,
When, only because in adorning
The autumn leaves you are so near.
What do you ask of me now, Lord?

Your richness now lies on the land.
What is it you are now forming?
Is it <u>something you lovingly planned,</u>
To decorate your world so grand,
As before you I silently stand?
I hear you come to me warming;
What do you hold in your hand?
Why do you ask of me this Lord?
To wait as a leaf in the sun,
Watching my veins tell a story,
A magical play never done,
Turning and changing as one?
Who's only to just have some fun?
I'll cling to the limb of your glory,
Green, turning as gold I'm spun.

<u>Little Leaf</u>

I once became a little leaf,
Dreaming on in listing grief,
That never left nor gave relief,
As I questioned my belief.
Upon a little twig so high
Casting glances at the sky,
I then swung higher to defy,
And asked the Lord, "When will I die?"
Softly came his sweet reply,

"Why ask you now with earthly plea
What is to come, what is to be?
As, hanging there on limb of tree
The golden tone you cannot see.
Do you not know what I saw you bring

To my tree the first of spring,
When beauty all around you rang
That of which the Angels san?"

To my silent question in a dream,
I saw the answer start to gleam,
Through October's frost and steam,
It turned into a flowing stream.
So casting doubt, I dreamed this much,
That I would never know of such,
The changing color from your touch,
As to the living branch I clutch.

"It is not you", You whisper tell
"You that grasps, it's I compel
And woo in love so all is well.
You did not buy nor can you sell.
As you came, so will you go.
I am the tree from which you grow.
Just see the beauty that I sow,
Then hush you made a wind to blow.
I would not drop you from my limb.
I the Light will grow not Dim.
I will make of you a hymn,
With rain and sun up to the brim,"

Listening, I fed on Him
"You cannot fall from my face.
You are caught up in my grace,
As everywhere and every place,
I am substance, I am space.
To see my sun you have not eyes,
But with my spirit I baptize.

So then the warmth from me testifies,
Until the time when your stem unties,
and you the little leaf falls and dies.
Then will slip your golden skin
down to earth in a swirling spin.
It is not earth's cold lap you're in,
Or beds for burning that you win,
A new life then you will begin,
A spirit leaf you've always been.
Behold your form now genuine,
Hangs on my tree of crystalline.
Behold my arms you lie therein.
My sun, your color truly burned
Into the color you have turned.
All that's useless now is spurned
And left is love for which I've yearned."

The Gleaming Answer's song was done
and still upon the twigs we hung,
Warmly cast the glowing sun,
While moonlit nights and daytime sung,
The color of the gold was spun.
Reflected in us as we age,
What grows within us does engage,
Unknown time to form in a clay cage,
The lasting cast of Love's Image.

I drove out of Alaska on October nineteenth, Kim's twenty second birthday, with all my belongings in the back of my station wagon. When I got back home I stayed with Mom and Uncle Leo for a few months. I also met up with y ex-husband Tom who seemed quieter, always sober and calm. I began to sense that he was weaker than I remembered. Tom died in 1992 and is the subject of my first book,

Something Loving Planned, (The title a phrase in the poem above that I wrote in October just before leaving Fairbanks.) I also lost others in my live during my first years back from Alaska. My First husband Ronnie, who I was always on speaking terms with for years, died a few years after Tom Then my sister, Ardis in her early sixties died not too long after him. Here is a picture of my sister who although we always lived so far apart I miss to this day. I will never forget her at thirteen, going forward and committing to Christ at that little brown church, and her courage, and bravado, when she just opened up and told dad after we walked home. She stuck to her guns, even though he scoffed a little, and I felt bad for her and never spoke up. She remained faithful to her church going all her life. And I was impressed with the holiness with which her pastor, a United Methodist, knelt and prayed for her at her bedside in the hospice facility where she was just before she died. It took her just the walk home to announce her acceptance of Jesus and walk with Him, but it has taken me many years to tell my story, in a way, it is part the walk I traveled on to receive Christ, and then the walk to follow Him; so, I am still on the aisle walking towards Jesus with the Comforter abiding.

A Picture of my sister Ardis
and me taken a few years
before she died

17 FLASHBACKS

This was one of the first incidence of flash backs, premonitions and portentous stuff in my life, that I had taken note of. For I met with Tom after coming home; and I found him finally sober but strangely weakened, and sick, then soon after he was diagnosed with AIDS. I took care of him for three years before he died. It was a time lovingly planned and my journal during that time became my first book. This episode was followed by my working as a nurse, having gone back to finish nursing school, and moving to Michigan to live by my daughter Linda, and her son Ronald. The Mass and church were back in my life, but there was no prayer group at the church where we lived. I missed the deeper things of the prayer meeting, the closeness and praising God rapt in the Holy Spirit. I still continued to go to mass, only frequently not regularly while working full time as a nurse on the swing shift.

In 1993 I sold the trailer in which I had lived, went back to nurses training, and taken care of my ex-husband Tom. I moved to Michigan and moved in with my oldest daughter Linda, who was recently divorced and lived with her for a year, because I wanted to babysit for my grandson Ronald while she was at work on the night shift. We both joined the Catholic church near by. In 1995 I bought a little house two blocks from my daughter and my single life began to be a joy. I worked as a nurse in a town near by and attended church as often as I could, taking my grandson with me.

It wasn't long though until in June of 2002, when sudden death and loss entered my life again. This time, it was my oldest daughter Linda who was killed in a horrible traffic accident, near Grand Rapids. I was completely devastated, more it seemed than before and completely heartbroken.

My life seemed unreal, and my grief so deep I would wake up in the morning groaning from down in my heart and lay down at night, withdrawing on a cloud of helplessness, but only after reading from all the books I drew around me like a comfort blanket. Those books seemed to be the tools to feed my soul strength because I had none, as there was nothing anyone on earth could say or do to give me consolation. Only God's consolation could suffice, as in those days of my conversion experience, only God can come to your aid in these times. But God's presence seemed to prevail in everything around me as it did when Kim had died, and I floated through those weeks afterwards, all the while the loss sunk like a giant ache deep down into my heart.

All my relatives flooded around me; for about a month, some even moved in for a few weeks and I thank God for them and all the support I received as I and all of them grieved greatly. I had things to do during the day, but in the morning the huge dark ache was pressing and heaving in my chest. My brain reeled with grief and confusion, a grief a kind of mental pain that is indescribable.

Every morning I groaned softly while my soul wept before I opened up my eyes waiting until the day happened to me; then again at night I would go to sit on my bed and the huge dark ache would threaten me again but, I turned to prayer to sink in thoughts of God. And almost as if on cue I would be compelled to find God; my thought flew to him. Hunger for Him filled my soul every night before bed replacing any despair found there and I hunted hungrily for my books, all the books that I could find that would possible feed and soothe my soul and I found them. Mostly they were the *Bible, My Daily Bread, My Way Of Life* (Saint Thomas simplified), and *One Day At A Time in Alanon,* a handbook. As I read these every night my thoughts were calmed, my soul replete with satiation and I felt strangely comforted. It was almost as if an angel sat beside me and relieved some of the wrenching loss I felt at the death of Linda. I will never forget it.

Although the book hunger and the feeling of God so close lessened the huge ache of loss remained but it was bleached out in its ability to press me with sadness. After a few months the thing that remained was a reluctance to get around and do any thing until the middle of the afternoon and this was unusual for an early morning person like me. I just did not want to face the day and preferred TV and or reading fiction for escape. That gradually wore off but it took having custody of my grandson, added time and handful of vitamins in the morning that I believed to help physical and mental well being. I carry Linda with me the same way I carry Kim very close to my soul. They abide in me, and I with them. People never get over the death of a child only live sort of beside it. You can't get past it; it goes with you. I know I will see them again after I die, the only thing is, that it is backward they went before me, but I will follow them soon.

I got custody of my grandson Ronald after Linda died and he was a great blessing and filled my life for the next few years, I can't really describe the great loss that I felt again losing one of my children; it's impossible to do so. It is impossible to describe life and living after losing your children so young. How one goes on, how one loves, how one finds anything to do that matters is beyond me; I just do it, that is all. I still can't wrap my mind around it and maybe God will show me how to do that some day. But it just can't be done now, not by me anyway.

I just live with it now, There is no other choice and God it seems has kept me busy writing. This conversion story has been at the top of the list since Linda died, but has had a hard time working up into the realms of my muse. I pray this effort here will please him. I lay it down before him, hoping this is what God wants me to do. all I want or desire to do is to write and write until I die. More comes in my heart almost daily to put to paper for Him.

18 PUZZLE PIECES

That is where I am at now for I cannot read enough, listen to enough catholic audio books, CDs, DVDs, or TV. I cannot think enough, or learn enough about the love of God. Help and Insights from listening and reading about all the saints and their writings, from early church history to present day Catholic teaching, astound me daily. I scour the internet and find the wealth of Catholic literature, prayers and devotionals wonderful. I am floating again at times but this time gaining affirmation and confirmation of God's love and His forgiveness. God permeates life, in and around me and in the entire existence of everybody in the world. Because of this I must add another small mystery of my story in conclusion.

Small pieces are continually found to fit into the puzzle that surrounded the events of my conversion in 1967. I list them here: a strange young man in the hospital ward at the same time as me, my missing comb, broken glass on the window sill, the two furtive men by the library, the night dream of the picture of Jesus and the morning spot of wax, and not the least of these, I add the mystery of my little cousin Gail, and Kim's being twenty one when she died.

    On my second day in the hospital, I first saw the young man whose hair I cut in the hospital back then. I saw him lying stretched out on the couch in the small TV room across from the nurse's station. He was long and his legs stuck out over the end of it and his arms rested behind his head on the opposite couch arm helping him view the room. Everyone there said that the police had just brought him in. He looked awfully familiar and I thought and thought hard trying to figure out where I knew him from. Then the next day I was again in the TV room in the morning and he was on the couch I was sure I knew him, his features were so familiar, so I studied his face again but this time I had a sudden flash; he looked like Billy Graham! And I told him that and that I had been trying to figure out where I knew him from. He said, "If you remember don't say." And that puzzled me, but did not stimulate my memory at that time. The conversation then went to his being there and that the doctor had released him depending on if he had a haircut. I asked the nurse about it and she confirmed what he said about the haircut, but said there was no way he could get his hair cut. They refused to do it and there was no barber available. When I heard that I felt sorry for him and I was so full of God's gift of love in my new heart that I said I would be glad to cut his hair for him, in order that he could be released from the locked ward we were on.

    I had cut my husband's hair several times, and my son's too, so I had no fear that I could do good enough to satisfy the condition set out for him to be released. So the nurses provided the scissors, (And this now amazes me because we were on a psych ward!) and I set about to cut his hair but had no comb to use when cutting it. His hair was shoulder length and snarled so badly that I really needed a comb to facilitate the cutting job.

Then to my surprise the young man, who seemed to own nothing in the world, whose clothing was dirty and ragged, pulled a nice white comb out of his pocket. I took it hesitatingly, and with a feeling of helpless wonderment, proceeded to cut his hair using the scissors that the psych nursed had provided and a comb amazingly, exactly like my missing, little white comb. The young man who I knew his name by then, but will not mention it here, sat quietly while I completed the job, which was not too bad a job at that either. It passed the doctor's inspection and he went home later that day.

I had so much on my mind then, and was so full of love, I can't remember giving this comb too much thought until another time, either a few days, or weeks later, or maybe a year later; I can't remember now exactly when musing, that maybe he had broken into my house that night causing the broken glass on the sill and took my comb from off the counter on the way out.

I also realized, when dwelling on the unusual event of the library men incident, that it became clear as a bell who the men were. The tall scraggly thin younger one with the hood on and only a facial features and profile, matched the Billy Graham young man in the hospital to a T. And the hunched over, heavier older one, with the hat brim pulled down, with only a nose and shadowed features of face showing, matched the preacher to a T. I was not accustomed to seeing him in a hat and a long trench coat but it is not a far stretch of imagination to think he might own such articles of clothing. Even today I would bet my life on the fact that the two characters burned into my memory exchanging something, maybe money and drugs in the library incident, were the preacher and the Billy Graham resembling young man. I just couldn't figure it out until after my life settled down with the comforting I had been given.

The next mystery to mention is the dream of seeing the

picture-like face of Jesus, and feeling the warmth on the spot over my heart. Well, I still don't know what to say or how, or what that could have been. But, I know I had wax on my breast over my heart that I peeled off, but could I have been hypnotized on the long car ride to the neighboring town that I took with the preacher, and that other man? I don't know but it is the best conclusion that I can come to, and if it happened that I was hypnotized in the car or in the night, I am even more thankful to God who watches over those who call upon Him. In the end, I feel no need to try to bother with the solution to that little remaining riddle about the wax, as it can be a mystery for as long as I live if it wants. All will be made clear some day, I am sure. The next piece of the puzzle teasing my mind, simply warms my heart.

19 LOOSE ENDS

    The portentous statement of my five year old cousin Gail still resounds in my memory fondly now, "If you are not Catholic you are going to Hell." Well, the way it turned out, it should have been stated, "if you memorize this Catholic prayer the Devil, and Hell will flee"!
    That day in the hospital ,when I was ushered into the place where I saw Mary kneeling beside Jesus and prayed the Hail Mary, the prayer rose, summoned from somewhere deep inside me, leaping to my mind, and on my lips, out from my abysmal torment as I scanned the bleak horizon dangling over the very horrible pit of hell. It was the Hail Mary that instantly crossed the gulf reaching Mary. For, no sooner was it out of my mouth, or maybe even in my mind she looked right at me and turned saying something to Jesus. Jesus turned to me and my heart and soul was flooded with the healing love, the cleansing flood poured into me

and my whole being, filling me up to overflowing with pure, clean, unimaginable love. And I remember and must recount again that this sequence was so instantaneous it was one. It happened all fully and entirely at once. All movements and actions were one, at once, a single unit of being.

And so now, considering and knowing what that Hail Mary prayer brought to my life, I am in wonder and amazement as I look back on that episode in my childhood when I was memorizing the Hail Mary. I can clearly see how God willed all things to be for my well being. And even the prophetic quality in little Gail's words were not my undoing, but at God's disposal for his glorification, for my good, and maybe for the good of all the people that read this book. Nothing goes unseen or unnoticed by God. I cried for mercy and he heard me, He heard me years before the real emergency, and provided the means for His mercy to come. He found a way to break through my defenses, led me through the horrible darkness by the light and the truth of His church, to a place where the comforter could enter and heal me. I could let go of any prejudices about another faith that I may have harbored unknowingly and any thoughts about Jesus coming because I figured he should.

I may have had to let go of any hidden distrust of women in general because of the abandonment by my own mother as a baby, and buried pain and distrust of the mother of God, Mary from long ago. I don't know but can say neither truth nor light are either relative or subjective and neither is Jesus and in the pure love of Jesus no anger, hatred, jealousy, or any evil can exist.

Jesus knew and in the intricacy and unfathomable wisdom of His redemptive work saw me rooting on that unknown shoulder. He, love and mercy itself, had been there watching me root on that shoulder. He watched and waited for me to ask the right person the right question so He could flood me with all the love he could fill into my heart. He drew me close to His mother and showed me to her and I saw her and asked the question the only question I knew. I needed help for my miserable condition and said "Hail Mary full of grace, Blessed are you among women and blessed is the fruit of your womb Jesus, Holy Mary mother of God, pray for me a sinner now and at the hour of my death. Then, He healed me with an everlasting love that stretched deep and far back to the beginning before I was born into the future even there is no end to his love it is unfathomable and eternal and not measured by time. She, Mary Full of Grace kneeling by her son watches over me too, my Mother.

  The last and greatest mystery is about the conversation with God when I was given to know that I would serve God when my daughter Kim was of age. For that is what happened I am aware now. Kim died when she was twenty one years old and I started the classes to be received into the Catholic church a few days before what would have been her twenty second birthday. But, that realization only came to me in bits and pieces at first for it a thought so poignant, so unfathomable and yet dreadful that I am in awe before even the thought of how vast is the immortal God I serve. For just more recently I realize that maybe it was God who pressed the words into me, that the thought was never mine; the thought, "When Kim is of age," was an answer to my plight of being completely dumbfounded as to what was transpiring. Our God is so kind, so thoughtful, so polite and so loving, that he stepped in and moved in my life way before I would even begin to understand my search for Him, and long before I would be able to have communion with Him the way I am blessed to do now. The gifts He gives are unsearchable, and deep.

  I have been so happy and blessed since I became Catholic and further more I have never taken psychoactive drugs since the blue ones I threw away in 1968; that is except for two weeks of an antidepressant I thought I needed when I wept so uncontrollable and long after Linda died. The weeping stopped after a week and I stopped taking the pills because they did not allow me to sleep normally. I have been just fine without drugs; I do take a lot of vitamins though. I like to stay as healthy as possible.

February 25, 2012 Journal entry

Oh my God I depend on you. Never let me leave you again. Call to me loudly if I falter or fall far from you. Oh my God I thank you for all your goodness to me and for watching out for me while I was on the wrong road. For you Lord see all roads, all hearts, and keep your eye on your children, although I will never completely understand why you never let me go. Oh my God, I fall down in my heart and bow flat down before your almighty, and all encompassing love, and His mercy, which is a bottomless pool that I wait and long for, to fill me again.

Oh, and I want to mention that I read every book I can find on the internet available on librivox and elsewhere written by the saints and mystics. I prefer the audio version but not exclusively. There is great reading out there now and great information and of course the scriptures I love especially the mass readings and the gospel shared there. My life has settled down.

Wait, this was the original last chapter but the next one follows. (I back up a little in time for the next chapter with a quick flashback to October 2011)

20 THE COMFORTER SPEAKS

A little leaf poem that is an entry written the October before I returned home from Alaska, and found my ex-husband ill with AIDS. is where I got the title for "Something Lovingly Planned." And, much to my surprise I was perusing my journal entries for an Idea for a title to this book, when I came upon another little leaf poem inspired the first of October last year. Here it is

October 1, 2011

It is October again, the first, and here I am writing again.
Oh, and I feel October in my bones, and it is as if those Octobers, all Octobers of my life, multiply their joy sometimes,
and stir around in my soul.

"Oh Little leaf you still flutter,
and struggle a little on the twig,
Oh, little leaf, hang on.
Hang on a little tighter to the strings
of love that tie you there.
I am in them; I am there
in the very air of October and
I love October in your soul".

Sometimes October's early darkness
brings a soft light in the morning
and I am called to bask in the glow
of a fresh and altered dew.
Then I long to enter the gate of November,
that awaits the ground dusted with winter snow.
Dust me again, Lord; oh dust me again.

    The comforter came that day in October when I was writing. I know that now and He gave me comfort that day, along with some strength that I did not know I would need until later, as it was just two weeks after that day that my beloved cousin Gail was diagnosed with pancreatic cancer. Gail, who I had grown up with, who I had been so very close to in the years since returning from Alaska, was desperately ill. I was devastated; how could this be happening to Gail who loved life so much and greeted every day with hope, even though she suffered with crippling post-polio. a disease that had kept her in a wheel chair for the last few years.

    She was kept at home to die as was her wish, and I helped her family take care of her for the two short months left in her life. I still weep when I think of her, but was grateful to share with her those last days. Mom, who Gail had been caring for in her home, had died just a year before. I grieve the family members in my life, but know I will see them again. And Gail touched my heart with her courage and will to live, and love, despite the hardships of her life, which she dismissed carelessly to the side, as if they did not even matter. She forged ahead regardless of being crippled, in pain, and in a wheel chair the major part of the latter part of her life with post polio. I watch the peace enter her and come upon her the last days of her life and she died a peaceful death with her priest praying the litany of the saints and other prayers for the dying over her.

    The blessed assurance I received those many years back has never left me. The Comforter is always near and even when I forget and wander off on a doubtful path, he abides, and brings me back somehow to be closer again than ever. I still get some chides when I am nudged to notice and regret something I said, and given a nudge to refrain, speak, or to correct a situation.

This was taken around Thanksgiving just before Gail Died. She was cared for at home; her smile was still sweet.

These last chapters are not the original ending and not chapters I ever thought I would be writing, but I am learning conversion is ongoing, for my story is not done yet. But the production of this book came to a complete halt in May 2012, when my daughter Ann needed me to go to California, due to a sudden crisis in her life. So, I dropped everything, and drove down to California, and spent almost two months. I had a wonderful time there, with my Daughter Ann, and her family. Everything was turning out better than we thought with the crisis. We went everywhere together and with so much time, shared much with each other in order to catch up after years of being apart, except for a few shorter visits. On the drive home I went by way of Oklahoma to spend a week with my son Arthur.

I do not know how the Lord leads me, but I know He does for I came to know about the significance of this trip itself two months afterwards. For after spending six lovely weeks with my daughter and a fantastic and rewarding week with my son, I woke up very early the morning on the last day of August and finally got up, then a little later, answered a phone call from my son Art's ex-wife, Rose. He had been viciously attacked in a home invasion about 3:30am that morning Oklahoma time. just about when I was getting up; he was in the hospital in critical condition.

21 HOLY IS HIS NAME

    He died a little after surgery from multiple stab wounds, and it was exactly two months after my visit. And again, the Comforter was at work in the days before my sons death occurred. because when I had returned from visiting Art, my morning prayers had changed, becoming more intense and focusing on a single person, Arthur. I felt an inner urging and need to pray for my son Art. I had sensed a lost and wounded spirit inside him, although he did his best to act happy and busy with his life. He took me somewhere every day and we enjoyed the time together what ever we did. He took me on a fishing trip with along with my grandson and his friends. We did not catch anything but the boys did. In the afternoon, the kids swam while Art and I still tried for fish and I just loved the entire time there at that lake. I have always liked to fish ever since my dad used to take me out on boat fishing for blue gills and bull-heads.

We went out for coffee one morning, and spent the day at a beautiful park some miles away where he and the boys went swimming in deep icy cold water pools interspersed with incredible rocky, waterfalls. It was a wonderful cool spot on a very warm Oklahoma day. We stopped in a small town on the way home and bought a huge pizza and we all filled up. Another day was filled with a fun and an interesting visit to a huge flea market where he bought me a gorgeous tee-shirt with Our Lady Of Guadalupe on the front and back. I am wearing it in the picture of us together included with others in this chapter.

On our last Sunday together he went to Mass with me, just outside of town. I knew he had not been at mass since his sister's funeral ten years before, and I was thrilled for his company, having had to go to mass alone for so long. He knelt praying a long time. beside me at the consecration of the Eucharist, and I felt his humility and love; I knew he was saying an act of contrition. When we got home he told his kids, who had not wanted to go with us, "I went to mass, and it felt like home!" There was an emphasis on the word home. Right after church we passed an estate auction sign. We turned around and went back to the auction to look, and then returned the next day to get the things we wanted at the last day's discount prices. I was deeply touched somehow for we spent an entire afternoon at that estate auction; he was tickled with the whole excursion. I think it was because it was something he was not used to doing for a long time, and me too.

Later he expressed a little surprise and satisfaction, when telling someone; that he even had a great time at an estate auction, something he had not expected. I just loved it. I bought him a beautiful down comforter, like new. and an antique crucifix made in France, which he proudly put in a place of honor in the house, to be seen when you came in the door. And, even his ex-wife Rose, who he was still friends with, came over to visit him, and came into the house to see the cool stuff.

I had the time of my life. Although all these things were great, and our time together was enjoyed by both of us, I picked up on a hint of sadness he seemed to carry. It showed in the look in his eyes when he did not know I was looking, the things he talked about, the small omissions, little frustrations, glossing over problems with the children, the small things, only a mother can feel are not right. His pain seemed to rest on my heart, so I prayed a rosary especially for him, with his picture in front of me or on my lap, every morning, from the time I got home, until the day he died. I would touch and caress the picture trying to comfort him with my prayer and thoughts.

On Thursday, August 30th in the evening, I went to the regular meeting of the prayer group I belonged to, Servants Of The Lord Jesus Christ, at Saint Catherine of Sienna in Portage, Michigan. What occurred that night at the prayer meeting was portentous but I would not know that until a few hours later, when I received the phone call from my daughter-in-law early in the morning.

Art Fishing June 2012

Art and me, June 2012

I am seen here with all but two of my grandchildren. From left to right are, James, Kim's son, Jacqueline & Savannah, Tony's daughters, Ciara, Art's daughter, Ronald, Linda's son, Brandi and Zach, Arts two other children and Nikita my Son Tony's oldest daughter next to me. My Daughter Ann's children, Carrie Ann, and David in California were unable to make it to the funeral.

My Ann and Tony

22 A TIME TO MOURN

For weeks at prayer meetings the main praise I had been praying when we sang praises, was holy, holy, holy Lord, holy is your name. Holy is your name. That phrase was ever on my mind and I would repeat it several times. I just loved to pray that phrase, and that night on August 30th was no different. I took a note card to jot down the name of some of the songs I liked so I could look them up on the internet and I had it handy in my purse; it is here beside me today. After a few praise and worship songs including Lord I lift up your name, and Glorify Thy Name, there was a time for silent prayer.

One or two people gave a word, and I was suddenly aware of the sensation that the walls of the chapel were shuddering and the room air was different. I prayed silently this question,

"Shuddering Lord? and got the affirmative thought and that the air was bleached, I said I was not sure what shuddering meant, but that I took it to be a prayer. and I read the following g that I had jotted down on my note card: "The whole room is shuddering, let us shudder in union with joy for the Lord is in the tabernacle and the air is bleached with his presence. Let us know He is near and let our hearts burn and shudder with love.

Right after that a friend spoke these words, "I took it to mean, weeping," for she had been given a scripture to read, and she read from Ecclesiastes these familiar lines from Chapter 3 verses one to eight:

There is an appointed time for everything,
and a time for every affair under the heavens:
A time to give birth and a time to die,
a time to plant and a time to uproot the plant,
A time to kill and a time to heal
a time to tear down and a time to build,
A time to weep and a time to laugh,
a time to mourn and a time to dance,
A time to scatter stones and a time to gather them,
a time to embrace and a time to be far from embracing,
A time to seek and a time to lose,
a time to keep and a time to cast away,
A time to rend and a time to sow,
a time to be silent and a time to speak,
A time to love and a time to hate
a time of war and a time of peace.

Quite often these words are read at a funeral, but that was not even on my radar. I could not imagine weeping that night, and wondered about what she had said about sadness. The prayer meeting continued on with more songs of praise, and a time for praying for those there requesting special prayers for a variety of problems.

I could not sleep through the night as I usually can of late, but that night I woke up three times, the last time was around 3;30am. I tried all the things that usually help me get back to sleep such as my book on CD, the sleep aid, acetaminophen and getting up for a cookie or a piece of toast as last resort. Nothing helped and so after tossing and turning for a while I got up about four twenty or twenty five. I rolled out of bed to my knees about 4:20 (3:20 in Oklahoma) because I felt wide awake but strangely troubled and in need of reassurance that prayer brings,

There by the bed my mind drew a blank as to what to pray about. but I felt like I should pray. After searching in my thoughts I could only come up with a little at that time in the morning, something of a short plea. I prayed a prayer of submission to Gods will. Oh Lord, I don't know what to pray, but Lord, I am yours, what ever this day holds I will accept. Help me go throughout this day doing thy will, and let all I do be pleasing to you. I walk in your day. And then, I got up to go to the kitchen to make coffee. I was just there in the living room with the TV on EWTN and noticed that one of my favorite series was on when the phone rang, I am not at all sure what time it was, but it must have been around 5am. It was Rose telling me what had happened to Art and the kids. She said Art had been stabbed and was at the Hospital but she was not sure which one.

I became frantic in my fear for Him and wrote in my journal. My family, my Son, where is he? while I tried to find the hospital numbers for Oklahoma city, Rose had mentioned Presbyterian and SW Med Center. But I could not find the one that had him, and not even the police could be reached. Finally, I called my daughter Ann, and there was no answer; next I called my Son Tony, and he answered. Of course the news I had to tell him was heart- breaking and terrifying, and he said he would find out where Art was and call me back. The time noted in my journal was five forty when I called him. That was of a great deal of help to me, and I started packing clothes and trying to pray, beating the air with my fearful helplessness.

I had some bags in the trunk and throwing more stuff in other backpacks when Tony got back with me about the Hospital and I called there for information but got nothing other that he was in surgery and they did not even know his name. They were not helpful because it was a police case due to the home invasion that took place. I told them Art was Catholic and asked them to call a priest. They said the chaplain would be in touch with me. I spoke to two operators the emergency personnel and all they could say was he was in surgery and the chaplain would call me.

Finally I found out that he was out of surgery and in intensive care, by then it was going on towards seven am. The intensive care nurse could give me no word about how he was except he was not awake yet and when I asked him to call a priest for Art he said the chaplain would be calling me. After that call, I suddenly realized I could try and reach a priest there if they had no priest to call at the Hospital. So, I called the priest in Mustang at Holy Spirit Church that we had seen at the mass that day. But he was just going in to mass and said he couldn't go just then, but would pray for him at morning mass and go to see him that day. I felt a little better then but that was not to last long for shortly after, I got the call from my son Tony; he told me that Art had died at eight o'clock and I noted it was just after I spoke with the priest.

23 ENTER NOVEMBER

Linda's son Ronald came down from Kalamazoo, and we left about noon for Oklahoma, with him driving, That morning the police caught one man running away, and the next day they apprehended another man and woman, who were also involved in entering my sons home and murdering him.

Art's funeral was a week later on the following Friday. The events of that week were filled but heartbreaking even in their precious moments, with almost all my family, Art's family there, and most of the grandchildren and my other son and daughter. We shared our deep grief and I will never forget it.

My prayer group friend's phone calls and prayers over the phone were of immeasurable support. I went to mass there and every one was friendly and helpful, a priest offered a mass for him in the rectory after services on first Saturday. The Comforter was at work and I realized in the middle of prayer one morning that what I had been trying to pray the weeks before the death was part of The Magnificat, "holy is his name", and what I had essentially prayed that morning when I rolled out of bed was similar, "I accept this day happenings according to your will."

This is all so fresh in my mind it is difficult to put down here and I have been stopping for a day or two between paragraphs. It's like it takes strength to write about it; and I want to write because there is something important to say, but I am not sure how to put it into words.

The title for this book may not seem like a title for a conversion story. But it is the one I landed upon when searching around in my journals that best fits the story I have to tell. For it is a journey from 1967 in the spring of my life, to this decade of my seventies in the autumn of my life. What awaits me, I do not know, just like any other person on this earth. I have come to know in a real personal way just how unsure we can be about the next day. I mostly live more and more by the hours of the day and thank God for the day's events as I go along. Every day I live is his day that I have entered. He it is, who knows the world and the people in it, and it is we who do not know the world nor why we are in it, although we carry on as though there is no end to it.

God has been with me from the start, and has never left me. I, on the other hand, in many periods of my life wandered far from him and then soon found myself scrambling back to Him. He is always there to give me reassurance in many little ways. It is he I must trust as no one else has an answer for any of the trauma, problems, pain, trouble, or illness in the world. I remember His intense and all encompassing love and how it permeated my very being, If then this loves rules, how can I but trust it to be true, just and forever working for my good, and the good of all in the world.

Only the creator and designer of such a marvelous universe would understand all in it from the hairs on my head when I was born, to the contours of my children s path that they took when they left me. I cannot see, or feel, nor touch with my hands where they went, but I know deep down that He does, and I trust I will see them again some how. I can't say someday because there are no days left after we die. I believe we go where we cannot even imagine the love and beauty or the bodies provided for us.

November 3, 2012 Entry

The other evening at All Souls Day mass, in my silent prayer I asked the Lord about my path again, and his will for me, I guess I just wonder about the things like, what should I do now? Do the things I do please Him? Did I choose the right thing to attend to? I then had a really wonderful explanation that answered my question but I could not right it down just then. I forgot about it until now the next morning after watching a documentary about Saint Edith Stein, and I am writing here about it in my journal. That program was fantastic; it was about trust and God's plan. Trust, unreal, for it answers some of my questions and now I remember the answer I received.

It is in this morning things, thank you Lord. For, yesterday after communion, my prayer was a lifted thought about, what do you want me to do now Lord? and I noted a heart whisper

"I will place it before you, in front of you; I will put it in your path. Just only hold me" (Bind me tightly, closely to your heart; however you can best do it, hold me there,)

So now I know I have to be always in trust, by trust, finding my way into trust and meeting every day as if on tightropes carrying a most precious cargo. It is a very fragile treasure that is the very source of our energy, and breath, and light for our blinded eye inside our hearts. Are your eyes there too Lord? Yes I believe they go daily with their purpose, that you do your will with these things I am given leave to do, things I am blessed to do, and am granted freedom to pick a path to walk on. May it be pleasing to you Lord, may you easily find me trusting and watching for what you may lay in front of me.

November 11, 2012 Entry

I am typing up a note for you Ann; I made it listening to a program on EWTN on the 11th of November. An African priest, Fr. Maurice Emelu, an author, was being interviewed; I took note of something that you might be interested in. Here is what he said about the Book: "Scaling the Heights " I jotted down, "When you get so comfortable, you forget God...You can find Him when you reach your discomfort point ...Confronting the reality of helplessness. .....Seeing the immense vastness of my unknowing, that impenetrable wall that shuts me down...... to a point of submission, to the almighty God above. (And there, I found He was There for me. where no one else could be.)

I also heard on the program, "Passing through the cloud of unknowing is a path of suffering. Bringing suffering to the foot of the cross....to the table of the Lord, ---laying it down in the bed of my life and sleeping with it, by trust...holding hands with trust....I write a lot of entries like the following in my journal and want to share this one.

November 12, 2012 Entry, The Field of Souls

Tilled by the hand of God
lies naked and bare before Him.
It is His land alone and only
He may work therein.

none other may pierce it,
none other may turn it over.
He goes in gently, with a whisper.
Only His breath may water
that thirsty soil and satisfy its
hunger for rain. Only He
is its tender, and only He
waits on its needs.
And even He will not enter
nor till until given leave. Then
Tenderly he goes forth with plow
bending the weeds away.
Softly He blows and the wind
spreads and drops His seeds
Love, across its fertile expanse.
He courteously waits for you
to invite him to enter softly,
deep into your eager soul,
fallow, hungry, dry, and thirsty.
He bends over the stony hardened land,
to tend the soil he created there,
for the garden of His Joy within us.
The garden He made for us,
to be with us, named Eternity.

November 23, 2012 entry

    I went walking this afternoon with my dog Spencer. He loved it and I did too, although it was a bit chilly, and then I noticed the faint snow falling. It was the dust of November, just in time. Heading towards December, the end of this year, and I still have not finished telling my entire conversion story. In other words, I have not really told why I chose the Catholic Church and converted to Catholicism. I need to tell you why in the aftermath and in the end of it all why I found the Catholic Church, and continue to find it to be the church my heart loves and cherishes

24 EVEN HE
Will Not Enter

nor will He till until given leave. Then, tenderly he goes forth with plow bending the weeds away.

    I found the title when looking for a fitting title for the last chapter. It is an excerpt from the last November entry and seems to sum up what I am trying to say.

<u>December 14, 2012 Entry, A December Ending</u>

    In conclusion, I need look back on those words created in my heart when I asked God about which church to worship Him in, and His Answer that came to me (with wonderment and chiding), "*Don't You Know?*"

    I realize now that He did not give me a direct, single answer of a name of a church, and not was anything further coming as I was somehow given or thought up an array of worshipers all praying, and the message about their prayers. I felt still a little at a loss as to what to do, feeling entirely so free to choose which way to go, and only His idea that I might already know, still seemed like a blank page before me on which I was to write. I only had my own feeble resources in the end and I was free to choose then and chose the Catholic faith without a second thought; I knew I was Catholic already. It didn't work out right away, but I never entertained any other church, and always had a peace in my choice. Perhaps I will never see fully the reason I waited so long to join, but a little light has come to me over the years, and recently many lamps have been turned on.

    I did not have reference, knowledge, or the tools to understand what happened to me back then or even the things I saw in the visions I was given. Were they of purgatory or hell? I am not sure which, but since reading about what the saints have witnessed and experienced has brought great understanding and solace to me. I have read the biographies of many mystics and saints who have had similar experiences. They had resources for the most part, and some had priests and other nuns to turn to confide in, or sought to join other religious persons in convents. From what I have read of their visions of hell, I have come to believe I saw purgatory when I saw the grey writhing people reaching towards Jesus.

    And I understand now a little about why He did not tell me right out which church to join. You see He is very gentle, loving, and polite. He will not force anyone to come to him; He only woos and guides and provides detours around obstacles and calls, and calls. He loves us so very much, that His love is unfathomable and He yearns for us to only love Him of our own free will. Free will you see, and I see now, is what he desires us to use in coming to him. He grants us complete free will in allowing Him to be in our life, to abide in Him, to seek union with him, and to come into His unsearchable love.

While in the beginning I used the reasons that it was the only church that honored Mary as its mother, held her in high esteem, and even advocated petitioning her for favors, and intercessory prayer. But also it was my husband's faith, even if he never attended in recent years. I felt somehow right taking his faith as mine. That was biblical from my learning about the story of Ruth, and Naomi, found in the old testament. I received great comfort from those thoughts and desires. There was a third reason too; and that was because it was the Church of Authority. I liked not having to be my own pope, find all the answers and figure out every little thing that Satan threw at me, to try to discourage or cause me doubt. I have hundreds of resources to read, the entire catechism to refer to if I have a question about what my church holds true; and there is the magisterium of the church that has studied more thoughts and question than I could ever think of. So in the end I did know and did choose.

And I think God knew all along, because He knew that I would come to see him in the Eucharist, that I would know and understand why Jesus said the things he said. And, One thing is in John 6:53, So Jesus said to them, "Truly, truly, I say to you, unless you eat the flesh of the son of man, and drink his blood, you have no life in yourselves." Now I know. No one explained before. I wondered about that scripture every time I read it.

And I believe Jesus, and what he said to believe in. I had read, and believed, and every thing I read, I found in the Catholic church. Everything I saw in the visions, and heard spoken to me, is in the Catholic church, and in the end I asked the same thing that Peter said in answering Jesus, when Jesus asked him something. John 6:66, As a result of this many of His disciples withdrew, and were not walking with Him anymore. 67, So Jesus said to the twelve, "You do not want to go away also, do you? 68, Simon Peter answered Him, "Lord, to whom we shall go?"

I want to say those words. often, only like Peter said them now. I want to be with Peter the apostle Jesus gave us to found his church, the one with 2000 years of bishops like him leading the followers of Jesus down through the years until now.

12/16/2012 Journal entry The Cloud of Loving Smiles

And in other words the question I asked was this, "Lord, to which church shall I go." So back then when I asked of the Cloud of love beholding me, that question, He may have heard the resemblance to Peters question "To Whom Shall I go?" The Lord may have been certainly smiling when he said, "Don't you know?" And, more curious is this: that I just noticed this similarity when typing this up on December 16th to finish this last chapter.

October has passed and even November is only an entry about the dusting of God's snow. For December has arrived with advent in full bloom. December, when Mary is remembered as the ark of the covenant, riding a donkey, carrying within her, the Bread Of Life, Jesus the living incarnate God. Oh Mary, thank you for hearing my plea.

Thank you Jesus for healing me, and coming with the father with the gift of the Holy Spirit, Who is like the wind, you cannot see Him, but you can see His work. Where the Comforter is He is at work comforting always. Comforting, the way He has comforted me over these past forty-five years, almost to the day. He has patiently been comforting, and very gently wooing, tilling the soil of my heart, and going gently, tenderly forth plowing, bending away the weeds.

Oh Lord may I always love greeting you in December and thank you for something that came when I was writing the other day trying to think of something to write in a Homemade card for Christmas for the elderly, *"I love December in your soul."*

Epilogue

I continue to journal most mornings, work on children's stories that I plan to publish and find time to walk my dog Spencer. I attend mass at my parish church and prayer meetings at Saint Catherine of Sienna.

In the Autumn while I was still working on finishing this book I found great peace in joining my prayer group on the 40 days for life prayer vigil outside the Planned Parenthood facility in Kalamazoo, Michigan. It was a rewarding experience and I hope to join the 40 days vigil prayers for life coming up in spring. Of course I wrote some prayers in my journal that came to me during this time and want to share one following this page.

Prayers For The Unborn

On my knees after the divine praises, I noted the scrolling sign
above and behind the iron fence. The first words were. We take
insurance. and I thought you *take only lives!*
The rest of the sign announce time, date, temperature and those
women over 50 could get help, and I thought:

Take yes; you take life-time from millions, temperature

experience from millions, dates, days, months, years
in the billions stolen, taken by you. And as for women
over 50 billions never made it to
50 seconds because of abortions.
Then I prayed, Oh Lord, holy mighty one,
fountain of life, you are living life itself.

You are the giver of life; I bind this sign
in the name of the Father the Son and the Holy Spirit.
May this sign come to speak only of your love,
and may all passing by see only Your words of life.
May it cease to serve abortions and serve only
You father, only shedding light for life of unborn.

I bind this sign over into the hands of Jesus,
in the name of the Father, the Son, and Holy Spirit.
Lord, Your mercy is more powerful than evil,
Lord you, the undying source and fountain of life,
You are life itself oh Holy Trinity.
Who can bind you? If they try they come only to fail.

For you are eternal oh my God of mercy, love, and life.
You are the immortal God of eternal life.
Thank you for this life you have given us.
We have eternal life that lives and courses through us.
Lord, bless these prayers that they may bring
justice to all unborn souls approaching abortion gates.

Pray For The Unborn

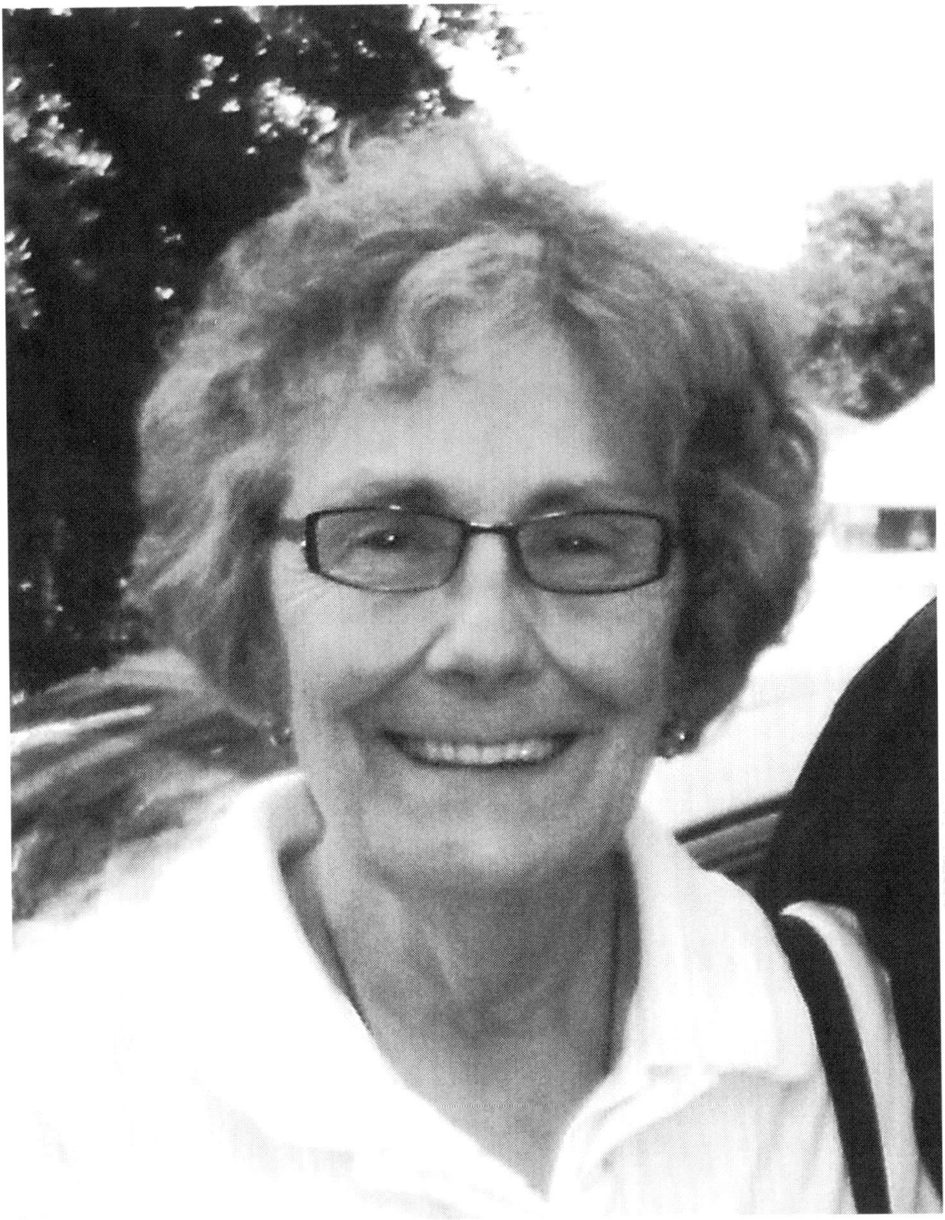

ABOUT THE AUTHOR

Sonja Carlo is a retired nurse living in a small town in Michigan. Journaling has been her hobby and main interest since first becoming interested in writing several years ago in Alaska, where she spent fifteen years with her family. She has three previously published books available on her website http://www.brownrabbitbooks.com. Go there for her blog and her books, Something Lovingly Planned, Paper Tongues Whisper, and a children's book, The Christmasmaker.

When God appeared to the author writing as a hobby or passion had not even entered her mind, but she felt a strong need to write it down on paper. So the first manuscript for this book was jotted down in a black hard cover book with blank journal pages to record the amazing conversion experience. It took a long time and much happened in her life before fruition of writing the full amazing story could come to pass. After several stops and starts the final rendition, is complete and available for all to read. This astounding account of events in her life, especially her experience with the Holy One and how her life was changed, is one you will find intriguing. The span of time between the initial conversion experience and the writing of this book is brought into the story, but as the author now will say; her entire story is not done yet and conversion continues to unfold before her. Consider how timely it is that the availability of widespread publication is ever so available now to people with a story to tell. And, this is one story that needs to be told now in these times of doubt, spiritual hunger, and turmoil in the world.

Other books by Sonja Carlo

Something Lovingly Planned, published 2011 by AuthorHouse
Paper Tongues Whisper, published 2011 by Sonja Carlo
The Christmas Maker, published 2011 by Sonja Carlo
The Willow Whistle, published 2012 by Sonja Carlo

Web Sites

Sonja Carlo http://www.brownrabbitbooks.com
Author's website tutor Sandy Fleming author, tutor, educator
http://www.allinfoaboutreading.com

Author's recommends the following public domain books which can be easily found at most book outlets on line or downloaded as audiobooks free on line, for study and as devotionals.

Author's Audiobook Favorites

Imitation Of Christ, by Thomas a Kempis at librivox.org
Revelation of Divine Love, by Julian of Norwich at librivox.org
Confessions, by Saint Augustine of Hippo at librivox.org
On Union With God, by Blessed Albert the Great at librivox.org
Abandonment to Divine Providence at Boston Catholic Journal
Abandonment to Divine Providence is also found on You Tube by a different reader and on cd available at some on line sites.
conversion stories can also be found

Conversion Stories

A few among many places where Catholic conversion stories can be found:

1. EWTN's library (Journey Home) also Journey Home You Tube.
2. The Coming Home Network
3. Why I am Catholic.
4. ConversionStories.org

Made in the USA
Charleston, SC
10 September 2013